INSIGHT COMPACT GUIDE

Bangkok

Compact Guide: Bangkok is the ideal quick-reference guide to this fascinating city. It tells you all you need to know about Bangkok's attractions, from its bustling markets to its serene temples, big-city modernity to timeless canals, and frenetic nightlife to more dignified rituals and dances.

This is one of 120 Compact Guides, which combine the interests and enthusiasms of two of the world's best known information providers: Insight Guides, whose titles have set the standard for visual travel guides since 1970, and Discovery Channel, the world's premier source of nonfiction television programming.

GW00707893

Star Attractions

An instant reference to some of Bangkok's most popular tourist attractions to help you on your way.

Temple of the Emerald Buddha complex p17

Royal Palace p20

Wat Mahathat p21

Vimarnmek Palace p33

Wat Pho p35

Khlongs p39

Chinatown p41

Erawan Shrine p46

Wat Arun p36

River Kwai p53

Pattaya p58

Bangkok

Introduction

Places

Culture

Leisure

Practical Information

Bangkok – a Challenge to the Senses

Opposite: flower market

Few cities fire the traveller's imagination in the same way as Bangkok. Golden temples, palm-shaded canals and classical dancers are just some of the evocative images that appear on postcards and in picture books.

Yet Bangkok is more than just a treat for the eyes. It is a sensual feast that envelops the visitor from the very first moment: tiny temple chimes tinkling in the breeze, an April sky filled with brightly-coloured kites, the aroma of chicken roasting at a roadside stall, fragrant garlands, incense smoke spiralling from a Chinese shrine, saffron-robed monks chanting ancient sutras in the morning light and, above all, the Thai smile and gracious manner.

Bustling Chinatown
Floral tribute

But not all the sights that greet the visitor are likely to prove so enchanting. Ribbons of concrete plunge like daggers through the city's heart, huge buildings dwarf the Buddhist *chedis*, and the sounds of a gentle people are lost in the roar of traffic. In fact, it is in many ways like any other modern city.

If Thailand is shaped like an elephant's head, then Bangkok is the beast's golden tooth. It is figuratively and literally the epicentre of the nation. With a population some 35 times greater than the country's second largest city, it dominates all political, commercial, religious and social activity. It is an island in a sea of green rice fields. Understanding it will help little in understanding the rest of the country.

5

What is it about Bangkok that fascinates visitors? Its colour, its chaos, and above all its contrasts. A range of cultural highlights that include temple architecture and sublimely graceful dances are counterbalanced by a nightlife that many find repugnant. It is a rowdy city – populated by tranquil people – which explodes around you, challenging your senses in a way few other cities can match. You are never at a loss for things to do in Bangkok. It is a hedonist's delight that can be explored on many different levels, from the exalted to the mundane. It is a city of rich and poor, of fragrances, flowers and the foul stench of stagnant canals. It is the pleasure of an afternoon by the pool and the discomfort of the searing heat that burns the air and bakes the pavement. Bangkok is a city that wins your affection without really trying.

Facing the world head on

Situation and size

Scarcely 30km (19 miles) from the sea, the sprawling city straddles Thailand's main river, the Chao Phaya. Its tributaries and man-made canals crisscross the low-lying delta like a huge net. Only 100 years ago, the waterways were the only means of

The modern face of Bangkok

Refreshment is at hand

transport. Lined by palm-shaded temples, shops and houses on stilts, they were used by boats of all shapes and sizes. Many of the old *khlongs* were filled in to create the broad boulevards. Like a giant octopus, the city spreads out into the surrounding countryside via these multi-lane highways. Even as far as Si Racha, Chachoengsao and Ayutthaya, some 80km (50 miles) away, industrial and residential areas emerge from the rice fields. Some 10 million people live within this conurbation, 6 million of them in the city of Bangkok. The city covers an area of about 1,500sq km (580sq miles).

Climate and when to go
Situated on about the same latitude as Madras, Khartoum, Dakar, Guatemala City, Guam and Manila (14°N and 101°E), Bangkok enjoys subtropical temperatures all the year round, but seasonal variations are brought about by the monsoons. The 'coolest' time of year occurs between November and February. This is the ideal time for a visit, but it is also Bangkok's high season. Between Christmas and the Chinese New Year, many hotels are full and the city's transport system is at full stretch. Temperatures rise rapidly from March to May at the time of the northeast monsoons, so the air-conditioned hotels and taxis are much appreciated. In June the southwest monsoons bring heavy rainfall and some relief from the sultry heat. Flooding frequently occurs in August and September, particularly in the area around Sukhumvit Road, and this can cause traffic problems. However, as it usually rains for only about two hours every day, it is still easy to explore the city.

Nature and the environment
At first glance, Bangkok seems to be an endless sea of houses stretching as far as the horizon. But stroll through the parks and the grounds of the international hotels or take a trip along the *khlongs* into the outer districts of Thonburi, where the coconut trees and fruit trees provide welcome shade for the wooden houses on stilts, and you will get a very different impression.

However, it is impossible to miss the excavators at work creating space for blocks of flats. The first tower blocks – many of which were built on the city's marshland – date from the end of the 1960s. Rapid economic growth during the 1980s and the subsequent building boom have taken their toll on the environment. The spongy soil has been compressed by the weight of the concrete and the surface has been sealed off with asphalt and more concrete. When the rain falls, the water does not soak away into the ground as it used to, but accumulates on the surface causing floods. In addition, the rising population

Flooding is a recurrent problem

makes ever greater demands on the water supply. Wells have been dug deep down to the water table with the result that this has begun to sink. Now the city, which lies only 10 metres (33ft) above sea level, is also starting to subside. During the rainy season, the newspapers try to predict if the streets are going to flood and when the city is likely to disappear beneath the sea altogether.

Another major problem is the permanent blanket of smog that hangs over the city. Policemen with face-masks try in vain to control the dense traffic, but the convoys of smoking buses, hooting cars, loud motor bikes and *tuk-tuks* never cease. Choking fumes and high noise levels cause most concern in the heavily built-up Chinatown district and along the main roads.

In 1998 there were more than 4 million registered vehicles in Bangkok, including over 1.2 million cars, 900,000 vans and light trucks, 66,000 taxis, 7,400 *tuk-tuks*, 1.6 million motor bikes, and 25,000 heavy trucks and buses.

Organised chaos

Population

Over 200 years ago King Rama I established the capital of the Siamese empire on the east bank of the Chao Phaya river. 'Bang Kok', the 'Village of the Wild Plum', began to grow dramatically. By the middle of the 19th century, it was bursting at the seams, even though the population was only 300,000. By the end of the century, the population had doubled. Nobody in their wildest dreams would have predicted another tenfold rise within the next hundred years.

Every sixth Thai lives within the Bangkok conurbation. The city is the trading and administrative centre of the country. Most of Thailand's industrial production takes place here, the best educational opportunities exist here and the highest wages are paid here. Bangkok attracts

A new generation

A gentle folk

the rural population like a magnet. During the dry season the poor from the northeast of the country flock to the city in search of work, usually ending up in the slums. The contrast between the poor day labourers and the ostentatiously rich elite could scarcely be greater. The economic boom of the 1980s produced a huge surge in opportunities for the educated middle classes working in administration or commerce, yet the demand for skilled workers cannot be met. Bangkok's illiteracy rate of 7 percent is one of the lowest in the Far East and nearly all 6-year-olds attend primary school, but only a third of them continue their education. Too few Thais possess the foreign-language skills necessary to take up the professional posts that the country is going to need in the future.

Traditionally the ethnic Thais, who make up some 80 percent of the population, prefer administrative jobs, which carry a higher status and also political influence. The Chinese community, the largest minority group (about 12 percent), dominates the business world, and not just in Chinatown. Unlike in most countries of southeast Asia, there is little tension between the Thais and the Chinese. Sikh businesses predominate in Pahurat, the Indian quarter; other minorities include Indian Muslims, Burmese and Vietnamese. Members of the hilltribes have also settled in the capital, where they sell their distinctive jewellery at the markets.

The Chinese

Chinese influences

Newcomers to southeast Asia find it difficult to distinguish between the different races, especially as people in the big cities rarely wear traditional costumes. Very few Chinese women, for example, opt for the traditional trouser suit or wide black trousers, and most young men prefer wearing jeans to the baggy shorts of their fathers' generation. However, during the Chinese New Year festivities, when many of Bangkok's shops close, it is suddenly apparent just how big the Chinese community is. For centuries, they have made up the overriding majority of traders in Bangkok.

Initially, the tolerant attitude of Buddhists and the fact that the ethnic Thais originated in southern China encouraged harmonious relations between the Thais and the Chinese, but tensions did arise at the beginning of the 20th century following a mass exodus from the Middle Kingdom. The new arrivals were accused of chauvinism and of exploiting the native Thai population. Their schools were closed and restrictive laws were introduced, denying them the right to own land and enter certain professions. However, this tension has since dissolved and the Thai Chinese are now fully integrated into their adopted country, and intermarriage is common.

Economy

Bangkok continues to be at the centre of Thailand's transition from an agricultural to an industrial nation. In contrast to the thoroughly modern capital city, rural conditions do not seem to have changed for centuries. While the production of rice determines the rhythm of life in rural areas, in Bangkok commerce and industry control the pulse of the city. While raw materials and foodstuffs used to be Thailand's main exports, finished goods and industrial products have now taken over. Fabrics, computers and semi-conductors are manufactured in enormous suburban factories.

The biggest source of hard currency, however, is tourism. According to official statistics, some 8 million visitors each year bring in the equivalent of 6 billion dollars. With the exception of those from Malaysia, most visitors use Bangkok as a stopping-off point and remain only a few days. Though their stay is brief, it creates valuable employment in hotels, shopping centres, restaurants and other service industries.

No-one can fail to notice that women make up a large part of the workforce. Not only are they the mainstay of the family, but they are equally at home working in the markets, road-building or in financial and commercial management. The figure of 80 percent of the country's women of working age in employment is the highest in the world. Not surprisingly, most Thais eat out or else take their ready-made meals home in little plastic bags.

Politics

Thais look back proudly at their great Chakri kings, Mongkut and Chulalongkorn. These rulers understood the importance of retaining the country's independence in the face of pressure from the European imperial powers of France and Great Britain. Instead of confrontation, they

Contrasting cultures

The royal coat of arms

Garlands for the monarch and the Throne Hall

opened up the country to Western influences, reformed the administrative system and created an infrastructure for the benefit of trade and commerce.

During and after World War II, Thailand's leaders adopted a pragmatic approach and a modern state evolved from apparently contradictory political forces. According to the constitution, political power lies with the people who are represented in the National Assembly, the Council of State and the judiciary. Elections are, however, dominated more by accusations of vote buying than by sound political debate. What results is often unstable multi-party coalition governments with the military playing an important part in the political equation.

Although Thailand has been a constitutional monarchy since 1932, the king still enjoys the respect of the people and can influence political matters. Every home has, for example, a picture of the royal family and, when the national anthem is played in cinemas, the audience stands to attention. King Bhumibol (b. 1927) came to the throne in 1946 and has, since then, witnessed no fewer than 19 military *coups d'état* or violent changes in government. He has won the support of the people by demonstrating his commitment to modern agricultural methods which, in theory, should help to alleviate rural poverty. His Majesty – the people have added the words 'the Great' to his title – is a unifying figurehead and this status has enabled him to intervene twice in the country's politics: once, in 1973, when he dismissed the military government and again, in 1992, when he forced General Suchinda to resign as premier *(see page 13)*. The rules regarding the succession have been amended, so it is now possible that instead of Crown Prince Vajiralongkorn (b. 1952), Princess Maha Chakri Sirindhorn (b.1955) will follow in her father's footsteps.

Prostitution and sex tourism

By the mid-19th century – long before the advent of tourism – Bangkok was already the setting for large-scale brothels. The brothel owners and customers at the time stemmed from the rapidly growing Chinese minority who had fled the crowded conditions of their homeland and came to dominate the trade and business world in Thailand. Thailand's entry into the modern world led to a further proliferation of prostitutes. As had happened in Europe, agriculture became unprofitable in many regions after World War II, and the peasants sank into poverty while a new middle class prospered in the cities. Suddenly one social group had money to pay for services of a sexual nature, whilst the others needed cash because their working skills had become worthless.

A burgeoning trade

During the Vietnam War, the American government chose Thailand as the rest-and-recreation centre for their armed forces because there was no shortage of entertainment of all kinds for its troops. The Thais, on their part, interpreted the behaviour of the GIs as an expression of modern Western liberalism, and so the progression from mistress, known as *mia noi* (minor wife) to masseuse and go-go girl occurred at breakneck speed. The result is plain to see. Aids is spreading at an alarming rate, and the government is stepping up its awareness campaigns to keep the public warned of its dangers. Thailand's anti-Aids programme is acknowledged to be one of the largest in Southeast Asia. Travellers who do not speak the language will not notice the stickers, warning signs, radio and television commercials. However, the results are only moderately effective in the face of a generation of Thai men who are conditioned into believing that regular visits to a brothel are good for their health. Meanwhile, the sex trade continues to proliferate, attracting customers of both sexes and every sexual inclination. Various figures estimate that there are between 200,000 and 2 million prostitutes in the country; what is more alarming recently is the spread of child prostitution, making Thailand a magnet for paedophiles from all over the world.

Thais in general are tired of their country's image as a destination for sex tourists, and the government is taking steps to reduce this unsavoury aspect of the country. Under existing anti-prostitution laws, sex with a minor under 15 is illegal. Sexual relations with minors are now punishable in many countries even if the act took place abroad. Cooperation between Thai and European law enforcers has led to a crackdown on foreign paedophiles. New legislation is aimed at increasing the punishment for those who sexually abuse, prostitute or procure children under the age of 18. The new law will also cover parents who sell their children to brothels.

Historical Highlights

1st century AD The Dvavarati culture – which comprises a number of Buddhist city states, mostly along the Chao Phaya valley – is founded by the Mon, a mixed race combining immigrants from the west (North India) and the original Thai peoples.

7–11th century The Khmers invade the country from the east (Cambodia) and penetrate as far as Central Thailand. Under their influence, Buddhism and Hinduism become integrated. At the same time, the Nanchao kingdom in South China blossoms into what was probably the first pure Thai state.

1238 Khmer power wanes and Thais led by King Intaradit establish an independent nation based at Sukhothai, south of Chiang Mai, marking the beginning what is now regarded as the Golden Age of Thai culture.

1277–1317 King Rama Khamhaeng develops the Thai alphabet. During his reign the country becomes a major power whose influence extends as far as South Thailand and includes parts of Laos and Burma.

1351 The kingdom of Ayutthaya is founded in the south, along the Chao Phaya river, supplanting Sukhotai. The first ruler, King Rama Thibodi, assumes the concept of a god-king (devaraja) from the Khmer. Traces can still be seen today in the wide-ranging religious duties of the reigning monarch.

1431 Ayutthaya conquers the Khmer empire centred on Angkor. It becomes one of the most prosperous and important metropolises in southeast Asia. The basis of the modern Thai state can be observed in its administrative and legal systems.

1511 Establishment of the first Portuguese Embassy. During the next 150 years, most European trading powers establish diplomatic missions in Ayutthaya. Siam becomes a world power.

1549–69 Seeking imperial expansion, Burma launches a series of campaigns against Siam. The Thais are defeated and the country overrun by Burmese forces.

1584–87 Prince Naresuan, since regarded as a Thai national hero, leads a successful revolt against the Burmese overlords and reestablishes the country's independence.

1657–88 King Narai allows Dutch and English companies to establish trading bases and the French to send missionaries. When Narai dies, all Europeans are banished.

1767 The Burmese destroy Ayutthaya. General Taksin is allowed to escape. In Thonburi one year later he declares himself king and begins to rebuild the empire.

1782 Taksin develops religious delusions and is executed.

1782–1809 General Phaya Chakri (Phra Buddha Yod Tahchulalok) or Rama I founds the Chakri dynasty. Bangkok becomes his capital and the Chinese inhabitants are resettled in Sampeng, present-day Chinatown. The Great Palace and Royal Temple are built.

1809–24 Under Rama II (Phra Phutthaloetia), many new temples are built in Bangkok. The first European envoys at the Royal Court take reports of the city back to the Old World. One very serious cholera epidemic in 1820 is followed by several more during the 19th century.

1824–51 Rama III (Phra Nangklao) signs trade agreements with the European powers. The first trading houses appear on the banks of the Chao Phaya. The expanding city (pop. 400,000) is secured by a third ring of canals.

1851–68 Rama IV (Mongkut) paves the way for modern Siam. National government is reformed and the economy expands. The Charoen Krung Road becomes Bangkok's first road parallel to the river.

1868–1910 Chulalongkorn, Rama V, opens up Bangkok to the surrounding countryside by building roads and railways. He reforms the education system and in 1873 abolishes slavery and serfdom. The city walls are pulled down and the rubble used for building roads. In 1883 a postal system along European lines is introduced. Telephones follow in 1886 and the first modern hospital (Siriraj Hospital) is opened in 1889. In 1894 the first tram runs along roads illuminated by electric lights. Many new government buildings and ministries are built to accommodate the growing number of civil servants.

1910–25 Oxford-educated Rama VI (Vajiravudh) continues his father's programme of reform. The irrigation system around Bangkok is extended. Britain persuades Siam to fight with the Allies in World War I.

1932 A coup d'état forces the monarchy to relinquish its power. Siam becomes a constitutional monarchy. The Memorial Bridge, the first crossing of the Chao Phaya, is opened.

1935 General Pibul Songkhram establishes the first military dictatorship. Ten-year-old Ananda Mahidol is crowned king (Rama VIII).

1939 Siam changes its name to Prathet Thai – Thailand, the 'Land of the Free'.

1941–5 During World War II, Thailand initially supports Japan in the conquest of Burma (now Myanmar) and British Malaya. Forced labour and prisoners-of-war build the 'Death Railway' to Burma. After the fall of General Songkhram and the Japanese defeats in the Pacific, the country aligns itself with the Allies.

1946 King Mahidol dies in mysterious circumstances. His younger brother Bhumibol Adulyadei accedes to the throne as Rama IX. He is not crowned king until 1950.

1945–73 At the end of the war, as the revolutionary movement gains ground elsewhere in Indochina, the country remains loyal to the western powers and the USA in particular. During the Vietnam War, the USA uses Thailand as a military base. Night-clubs for war-weary American soldiers open up in Bangkok and Pattaya. A power struggle between the generals and civil politicians dominates internal politics. Coups d'état and changes in government follow. The first multi-storey blocks are built in the 1960s.

1973 Bloody battles between students and the army bring about the resignation of the military government. Sanya, rector of Thammasat University, becomes prime minister. Political parties

are permitted again and King Bhumibol proclaims a new, liberal constitution. The first attempts to bring some order to Bangkok's streets with overpasses and traffic-light free junctions end in chaos. Bangkok's first tourists arrive.

1976 The military assumes power again.

1980 General Prem Tinsulanonda replaces General Chamanand in a bloodless coup. He rules in tandem with various coalition governments and survives several attempts to unseat him.

1982 Bangkok and the Chakri dynasty celebrate their 200th anniversary. Many buildings, including the royal palace, are restored to commemorate the occasion. The royal barges take to the water again after many years.

1988 Prem resigns and is replaced by Chatichai Choonhavan. Tourism records a rapid growth rate and becomes an important factor in the economy. Over 4 million visitors stop off in Bangkok.

1991 New, taller tower blocks are built and huge, suburban settlements spread out into Bangkok's hinterland. Inflation, the widening gap between rich and poor and instances of corruption in high places lead to expressions of discontent. The military assumes power again, overseeing a civilian government led by Anand Panyarachun.

1992–3 Parties close to the military win the March 1992 election. General Suchinda is appointed as premier and violently suppresses demonstrations which follow. The king forces Suchinda to resign. Democratic parties win the September 1992 elections; a coalition led by Chuan Leekpai seeks to improve standards of civil and military transparency.

1995 A new constitution is adopted. The Chuan government collapses, replaced by a coalition under Barnham Silaparcha, leader of the Chart Thai Party. General Chavalit Yongchayuth becomes prime minister following November election.

1997–9 On 2 July 1997, the Bank of Thailand's US$23 billion defence of the Thai baht fails; devaluation, economic collapse setting off Asia's economic crisis and Chavalit's resignation follow. Chuan returns to power and Thailand moves uncertainly towards the 21st century.

Royal Palace roofs
Preceding pages: Temple of
the Emerald Buddha

Lak Muang Shrine

Route 1

Around the Sanam Luang

Wat Phra Kaeo and the Royal Palace – Wat Mahathat – National Museum

To anyone who stands on the Sanam Luang, a huge oval area ringed by busy roads, and looks around, it quickly becomes apparent that this is the heart of Bangkok. Behind the high walls rise the gleaming gold towers of the Royal Palace and the Wat Phra Kaeo. In the adjoining Lak Muang shrine lies the city's foundation stone and the huge National Museum is home to the country's cultural heritage. Three universities border the only large, open area in the city centre, sometimes known as the 'Royal Field'. Families come to picnic here, students, women, market traders and office workers gather during the late afternoon, some to chat, some just to relax and watch the world go by. Both children and grown-ups come here to fly their kites – competitions are held here during the kite-flying season. It will take a full day to complete the suggested tour.

At the southern end of the field is the small ★ **Lak Muang Shrine ❶**, where the people of Bangkok come to worship the pillar built to celebrate the founding of the new capital city. All distances in Thailand are measured from this phallic monument, which receives daily supplications and countless offerings from the faithful. A *mondhop* topped by a *prang (see page 62)* has been erected above the foundation stone which is wrapped in brightly-coloured material and covered in gold leaf. The adjoining shrine is the home of Bangkok's guardian spirit, to whom flowers, incense sticks and other items are offered.

Visitors buy birds, turtles and eels and then release them in order to buy goodwill for the next life. They also buy a lottery ticket, in the hope that the spirits will bring good fortune in this life. To the delight of the spirits and the tourists, worshippers commission Thai dancers in heavy brocade costumes to perform traditional dances with some unusual accompaniments.

★★★ *Wat Phra Kaeo* ❷ *and the* ★★ *Royal Palace* ❸

This crowning glory of Thai temple art, a riot of gold and marble, will impress even the most jaded traveller. Respect should be shown at this hallowed site and appropriate dress worn – the guards will turn away anyone wearing sleeveless shirts, shorts or 'thongs', but will, if necessary, lend suitable clothing. A tour takes at least an hour. There are a number of pavilions where visitors can have a rest or stop to look at the features in more detail, and refreshments are available. It is open daily 8.30am–3.30pm. Taking photographs in the *bot* (inner sanctuary) of Wat Phra Kaeo and the palace rooms is forbidden. Included in the entrance fee are a guidebook, plan and access to the Royal Thai Decorations and Coin Collection and the Vimarnmek Palace (keep the coupon; *see page 33*). A website with information on Thailand's major palaces, written in cooperation with the Bureau of the Royal Household, is at www.palaces.thai.net.

Protecting the hallowed site

When, in 1782, Rama I decided to move his residence to the east bank of the Menam Chao Phaya, the area he chose, which became known as Rattanakosin, was the highest area of land and therefore the safest from flooding. The Chinese traders who lived here were despatched to Sampeng (*see page 41*). Rama's successors added further fine buildings to the original structure and decorated the existing ones in contemporary style. The **Gate of Victory** leads off the Sanam Luang into the guarded inner temple grounds which lie behind a tall, white wall. Some people may like to visit the **Royal Thai Decorations and Coin Collection** here with its old coins, orders and decorations awarded by the royal court, but most head straight for the west gate and the royal temple.

Wat Phra Kaeo

To commemorate the destroyed royal city of Ayutthaya, Rama I commissioned the construction of the magnificent 55-m (180-ft) long **Bot of the Emerald Buddha** to provide a fitting home for the most sacred of Thailand's Buddha figures. The three-tier roof rests on rows of tall, slender pillars,

*Temple of the Emerald Buddha:
exterior details*

which, like the facades, are decorated all over with colourful faience. A relief at the base shows 112 *garuda* figures warding off *naga* serpents with their hands; the birds appear to be supporting the weight of the building. Bronze lions in Khmer style guard the gates; of particular interest is the magnificent mother-of-pearl inlay work in the wings of the entrance. The venerated **Emerald Buddha**, a source of many myths and legends, can be seen inside, on an 11-m (36-ft) high golden altar beneath a nine-tier canopy surrounded by more splendid Buddhas.

The 75-cm (30-inch) seated Buddha figure made from milky-green nephrite, a type of jade, was the most valuable piece of booty that General Taksin brought back to Thonburi from Laos over 200 years ago. The capture of the legendary statue was visible proof of the increasing power of the young empire and its new dynasty. Even before the construction of the royal palace, a temple was built in its honour and the site named Rattanakosin or 'the place of the jewel Buddha'.

According to one chronicle, the priceless statue was discovered in 1464 after lightning struck a *chedi* – a monument erected to house a Buddha – in Chiang Rai. Hidden under a layer of dust, it was concealed from potential thieves. When the king of Chiang Mai sought to take it to his kingdom on the back of an elephant, the animal refused to budge. The elephant's stubbornness was seen as the judgement of god, so a temple was built at the precise spot where the elephant stood (in what is now Lampang). Some 32 years later, King Tilok brought the

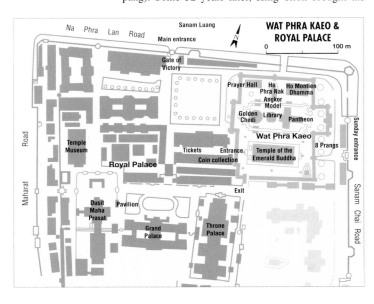

Emerald Buddha to the Wat Chedi Luang in Chiang Mai. When, in the middle of the 16th century, Chiang Mai fell to neighbouring Laos, the precious Buddha was taken to the Luang Prabang royal court and later to Vientiane where it remained until the Siamese conquered Laos in 1778. This Buddha statue in Wat Phra Kaeo still enjoys a position above all other Buddha figures and receives special adoration from the faithful. At a solemn ceremony held three times a year – at the beginning of the cool period, the hot period and the rainy season – the king or his regent changes the Buddha's gown.

The two bronze figures dressed in jewel-studded royal robes on either side of the Emerald Buddha are dedicated to the first two kings of the Chakri dynasty. The fascinating frescoes visible on the *bot*'s interior walls *(see page 62)* illustrate the Buddha's life cycles and are of great artistic merit.

North of the *bot*, a wide staircase leads up to a marble terrace, where three important, but completely different temple towers stand. A *prang* on a four-tier saddleback roof dominates the cruciform **Royal Pantheon** *(Prasad Phra Tepidorm)*. Mythical half-man, half-bird creatures *(kinara)* and two gold *chedis* adorned with figures of monkeys and demons guard the entrance. The pantheon, housing life-size statues and the ashes of the Chakri kings, is decorated with blue and red faience. The only days when the inner room is open to the royal family is Chakri Day (6 April) and Coronation Day (5 May). Behind the pantheon rises the filigree, pyramid-shaped *mondhop* roof of the **Library** *(Phra Mondhop)*, an almost square, richly gilded edifice. It is here that the sacred writings of Theravada Buddhism are kept. In each corner sit huge, central Javan stone Buddhas (14th-century), which form a contrast to the light, fanciful architecture. Next comes the **Golden Chedi** *(Phra Si Ratana)*, which Chulalongkorn had built above a relic of Buddha as an exact replica of the Wat Chedi Si Sanphet in Ayutthaya which was destroyed by the Burmese. It is surrounded by white elephant monuments, for centuries symbols of royal power. To the north of the library, a **stone model** of the Khmer temple complex at Angkor Wat, a present from King Mongkut, gives some impression of the sheer size of the biggest temple in southeast Asia.

Beneath the terrace lie the **Prayer Hall** *(Phra Viharn Yot)*, whose floral and blossom ornamentation in glazed china clay gleams in the sun, together with **Ho Phra Nak**, a mausoleum for members of the royal family, and **Ho Montien Dhamma**, the royal library.

After taking a break in one of the 12 small pavilions *(salas)* around the *bot*, there may be time to take a close look at the details: exotic-looking mythical creatures, the

19

The Golden Chedi, with demon

The Throne Hall

revered doctor on the plinth behind the *bot*, the 12 giant temple guards or *yaks*, and the long line of eight, differently coloured **prangs** on both sides of the east wall.

Do not leave the temple before making a tour through the **cloisters** which surround the temple compound. Colourful frescoes, starting at the western entrance, retell the Ramakien legend *(see page 63)*. The story ends by the southwest gate, which leads into the Grand Royal Palace.

The Royal Palace

Just a few yards away stands the 'Grand Residence' (Maha Montien); only the front section of the **Amarinda Throne Hall** (Amarinda Vinichai) is open to the public. Initially, Rama I's court of justice met here, but the dignified hall, maintained in pure Thai style with ornamental ceiling and wall paintings, was later used in coronation ceremonies. At state functions the king sat beneath the nine-tier canopy on an ornate throne, decorated with gilded carvings and glass inlay work. In the **Paisal Hall** to the rear, Rama I gave audiences to visiting dignitaries but, in later years, the kings were actually crowned here. The first two Chakri kings resided in the adjoining third building, the **Chakra-bat Phiman**.

Behind the small gate once lay the strictly guarded royal women's chambers and they are still reserved for the royal family. A ruler's power was measured by the number of his descendants, so there must always have been plenty of activity behind the walls. King Mongkut had a harem with 27 royal wives, 34 concubines and 74 noble women. Some sources believe these figures to be too low and suggest a figure of around 600 women and concubines would be more realistic.

The centrepiece of the palace complex, the **Grand Palace** (Chakri Maha Prasad) of the Chakri dynasty, was

The Grand Palace

planned in 1880 by Rama V as a royal residence in Renaissance style but, after an outcry within government circles, it was topped, not with domes, but with Siamese spires, guarded by upright *naga* serpents and three towers – an astonishing sight. Beneath the central tower lie urns with the ashes of all the kings since Rama IV; the other towers contain the ashes of lesser members of the royal family. A double staircase flanked by elephants leads up to the reception hall. Apart from a collection of weapons on the ground floor, the interior of the palace is not open to the public.

The delightful **Abhorn Phimok Prasad Pavilion** to the west of the Grand Palace was built by King Mongkut as a dressing-room pavilion. The elegant architecture is so typical of Siamese temple design that a replica of it was built for the Brussels World Fair in 1958.

Dusit Hall

The cross-shaped **Dusit Maha Prasat** stands behind it on a marble terrace. It was here that Rama I was crowned but, since his death, all kings of Thailand have lain in state here during the funeral service. A nine-tier *chedi* caps its steep roof; huge *garudas*, the vehicles of the god Rama, guard the gables. During visits by dignitaries, Rama VI took his place on the verandah in the covered *busabok*, a type of throne.

Take a break for refreshments and then head north to the Wat Phra Kaeo **Temple Museum**. On the ground floor, an exhibition illustrates the extent of the restoration work that was completed in 1982, while, on the first floor, votive offerings to the Emerald Buddha are displayed. Other exhibits include Buddha statues, glass vessels, porcelain and inlay work. Javan stone Buddhas from the 8th and 9th centuries flank a replica of the Manangasila throne of the nation's founder, King Ramkamhaeng. A large screen dating from the time of King Mongkut is a fine example of Thai-style lacquering.

To the northwest, a road lined with market stalls runs between the palace compound and the **Silpakorn University**, Bangkok's fine arts university, as far as the Ta Chang, a pier on the Menam Chao Phaya. As well as the express boats, *khlong* boats from the Khlong Bangkok Noi also use the pier. However, there is still much of interest to be seen around the Sanam Luang, so it is best to continue northward on foot.

Wat Mahathat and student

The **Wat Mahathat** ❹ occupies a site that was a shrine during the Ayutthaya period but this was destroyed by fire in 1782. The temple was rebuilt and, during the early years of the 19th century, it developed into an important teaching and meditation centre. A large part of the complex is taken up by the monks' quarters and lecture rooms. Crammed into a smallish space are the *mondhop*, the rather

plain temple *bot*, the largest in Bangkok, and the *viharn* (assembly hall). English-speaking monks are always on hand and are happy to talk to visitors. The meditation department (section 5) is open to foreigners (*see page 67*).

To the east of the *wat*, the ochre-coloured **National Library** houses interesting old manuscripts, books and inscribed stones, while to the north of Phra Chan Road, which leads to the jetty for boats to Thonburi station, you can stroll through the extensive grounds of **Thammasat University**, one of the city's largest and most respected seats of learning. Arts students here have played an active part in the recent political disputes.

For an overview of the cultural history of Thailand and its neighbours there is no better place than the ★★ **National Museum ⑤** (Wednesday to Sunday, 9am–4pm). The hour-long guided tours in English (Wednesday and Thursday, 9.30am) are free and it is well worth arriving early for them. Just past the ticket office to the left of the main entrance, an exhibition provides an introduction to the nation's past. The adjoining **Prehistoric Collection** consists of finds from the excavations of Stone Age sites in Kanchanaburi and pottery from Ban Chiang. (The museums *in situ* usually only have replicas.) The small **Red House**, a traditional teak house where princesses and concubines once lived, has been rebuilt in the museum garden. Its furnishings give some insight into the domestic life of the royal household.

Opposite the main entrance stands the small **Wat Buddhaisawan** royal temple, whose interior walls are adorned with fine murals depicting the life of Buddha. Its greatest treasure is one of the three Sihingh Buddhas (the two others are to be found in Chiang Mai and Nakhon Si Thammarat). All three can claim to be authentic. According to legend, the images date from the early years of Buddhism and were made in Sri Lanka, but some researchers believe they originated in the 13th century.

The older section of the central building was formerly the residence of the vice-king. The old throne and audience rooms (**4–15**) now contain exhibits, most of which date from the Bangkok period.

 4 Temporary exhibitions;
 5 Gold and jewellery from the Ayutthaya period;
 6 Decorated litters and *howdahs* (elephant seats);
 7 Khon masks, puppets and toys, including a doll's house;
 8 Pottery from various periods; in the gallery, mother-of-pearl inlay work;
 9 Ivory: tusks from famous elephants, carvings;
10 Weapons, fighting elephant's livery;
11 Royal insignia;

12 Inscribed stones;

13 Wood carvings, including the temple doors of Wat Phra Kaeo and Wat Suthat, the work of King Rama II himself;

14 Textiles: cloth, weaving and dyeing techniques, including recent developments; in the gallery, Buddhist objects;

15 Traditional Thai musical instruments.

The National Museum

This older building is surrounded by a modern, two-storey complex. The exhibition halls in the south wing contain *objets d'art* from the early southeast Asian empires:

S3–5 Early Hindu deities from Phimai, Prachin Buri and Srithep;

S6 & 7 Buddha statues and other religious objects in Dvaravati style;

S8 Sculptures from central and eastern Java (7–11th century);

S9 Works of art dating from the Srivijaya period in the south.

In the north wing:

N1–4 Sculptures, pottery, textiles and coins from the Bangkok period;

N5 Two giant, bronze Buddhas from the Chiang Saen period;

N6 Works of art from the Lanna period in the north;

N7 & 8 Sculptures from the Sukhotai period (13–15th century);

N9 & 10 Works of art from the Ayutthaya period.

On the first floor of the adjoining **Issaretrache Nusorn Hall** is a rare opportunity to see the furnishings of the old royal chambers.

Head back towards the main entrance and pass a large hall, where a number of royal hearses and litters are kept.

The **Silpakorn National Theatre ❻**, to the north of the National Museum, puts on popular plays and classical dances (*see page 64*).

National Theatre

Visitors to the **National Gallery** (Wednesday to Sunday, 9am–4pm, closed on public holidays, tel: 281 22 24), on Chao Fa Road, first have to cross the wide and extremely busy Somdet Phra Pin Klao Road. Temporary exhibitions staged by the gallery are usually worth a look.

On the east side of the Sanam Luang, the **Thorani Fountain ❼** represents the Indian earth goddess. According to the legend, Thorani saved the meditating Buddha from the temptations of the demon Mara. Every evening (except Thursday) a sale of secondhand clothing and other items takes place on both sides of the **Khlong Lord**, which lies to the east of the fountain.

Route 2

The temples in the east of the city

Wat Ratchabophit – Wat Suthat – Wat Theptida – Golden Mount

Central Bangkok between Menam Chao Phaya and Khlong Banglampoo, a semicircular area around the Royal Palace, was christened Ko Rattanakosin, meaning 'the place of the jewel Buddha'. Here the atmosphere of old Bangkok survives and plenty of surprises lie in store for anyone who takes an early-morning stroll, preferably on a Sunday or a public holiday when the traffic is relatively light. During the week, it is possible to take a detour through the narrow lanes and past long-established markets, and so avoid the overcrowded main streets.

Images at Wat Ratchabophit

24

Around 1870, not far from Khlong Lord, King Mongkut built the ★ **Wat Ratchabophit** ❽. All visitors to the temple come under close scrutiny from the carved soldiers at the entrance. The temple's tall *chedi* is enclosed in a circular cloister covered in yellow tiles. A Lopburi Buddha beneath the protective *naga* serpents meditates in one of its niches. A *bot* (in the north) and three *viharn* look out from the *chedi* in all directions. Finely-detailed mother-of-pearl inlay work decorates the doors and windows of the *bot*, as *garuda* figures and a seven-headed elephant look down from the gables. On the facades, china faience painted with floral motifs and heavenly nymphs *(devadas)* gleams with gold. In the courtyard of the temple's southeastern section, alongside numerous stone Buddhas, stands a memorial stone – the unassuming tombstone of Chu-

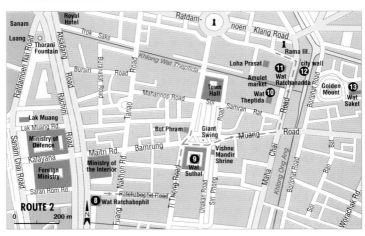

lalongkorn's wife. Access to further royal gravestones in the west is closed off, but it is possible to catch a glimpse of the cemetery from Atsadang Road. Among the Thai, Khmer and Hindu monuments are two attractively painted chapels in Italian Gothic style.

The route to the Wat Suthat leads through a series of narrow lanes, lined by traditional, two-storey shop buildings which are reminiscent of old Chinatown. Here, around the open square in front of the faceless **City Hall,** the Brahmin traditions are more evident than anywhere else in the city. After defeating the Khmer empire, the Ayutthaya kings adopted numerous rites from pre-Hindu times. To this day, watchful Brahmin priests ensure that they are carried out properly. One of the most dangerous rituals, the Swing Festival, was stopped in the 1920s after a number of fatalities. However, the red **Giant Swing** (Sao Chingcha), made from huge teak trunks in the time of King Rama I, is still visible. For the Tri Yambahva Festival in honour of the god Siva, teams of young men would set the swing in motion. When it reached a height of about 25m (82ft), one of them would try to snatch a bag full of money with his teeth from a bamboo pole some 20m (65ft) away.

The ★★ **Wat Suthat** ❾, one of the finest temple buildings of the Bangkok period, is home to the famous Buddha Sri Sakyamuni which once graced Sukhotai's Wat Mahathat. Work on the temple started under Rama I, but the door to the 30-m (98-ft) high *viharn* on the north side of the three-tier terrace was not big enough for the statue. The shrine was finally completed under Rama IV. The 6-m (20-ft) high gilded bronze statue (14th century) rests on a tall lotus plinth in which the ashes of Rama VIII are entombed. To the rear of the statue, **scenes from the life of Buddha** are carved on a 2.5-m (8-ft) high stone slab in Dvaravati-style. Lively frescoes from the first half of the 19th century, painted in rich reddish shades, cover

Inside Wat Suthat and outside Wat Ratchabophit

The Giant Swing

Wat Suthat: interior frescoes

Garlands at Wat Suthat

Bamrung Muang Road

the interior walls and columns from floor to ceiling. There are few temples in Thailand where paintings of such quality can be admired. They tell of the 24 legendary Buddhas who preceded the historical Buddha. It is unusual in a Buddhist temple to see – depicted on the door and window shutters – gods from the Hindu pantheon and the heavenly city of the god Indra. The three-dimensional wooden carvings on the heavy wings of the almost 6-m (20-ft) high doors are said to have been the work of Rama II, but some of the scenes from the *Ramayana* epic are replicas.

Across from the *viharn* stands the great *bot*, whose entrances are guarded by figures of soldiers dressed in European-style uniforms. Set out on the lower level of the terrace are bronze horses, marble pulpits, pavilions for the *bai semas* (border stones) and Chinese stone pyramids. The gable ends of the four-tier roof are extravagantly decorated with **religious symbols** and a three-headed elephant, while, inside, the life of Buddha is depicted.

Further Chinese sculptures can be seen in the inner courtyard – mainly ship's ballast that was left behind in Bangkok when rice was loaded on to junks. This temple has close associations with Rama VIII, who requested that his remains be buried here. A bronze memorial can be seen to the north of the *viharn* and every year on 9 June a royal ceremony is held in his honour.

To the northwest of the Giant Swing stands the Brahmin **Bot Phram**, which was built in honour of Shiva, Vishnu and Ganesha and his brother Skanda at around the same time as the Wat Suthat. The upper priestly caste from southern India was responsible even in Ayutthaya for carrying out the many Brahmin ceremonies at the royal court. The temple sees a constant stream of worshippers who come to pray, light candles and offer garlands.

East of the Wat Suthat on the Unakan Road stands the smaller **Vishnu Mandir shrine**, which is dedicated to the Hindu god Vishnu.

Follow the **Bamrung Muang Road** east, passing little shops that are stocked full of devotional items. Bronze Buddhas, sacrificial bowls, the orange robes worn by monks, life-sized statues of the Chakri kings and Hindu gods can all be bought here.

The necklaces worn by many Thais as talismans are sold at the nearby **amulet market**. This covered market is situated on the other side of the *khlong* beyond the **Wat Theptida ❿** with its faded Chinese porcelain decorations. Experts pore over the little beads which offer protection against disease, car accidents and the evil eye. The decaying, overgrown *mondhop* in which the haggling takes place is part of the **Wat Ratchanadda ⓫** temple site. The *bot* here is flanked by two small *viharn* and ringed by a double row of *bai semas* decorated with elephant pictures. Behind the *wat* is one of Bangkok's most unusual structures, the **Loha Prasad**. On three of the five square terraces, little towers are crowned by iron spires (the name means 'metal spire'). A network of tunnels runs through the square bases like a chessboard and, where the cool passages meet, monks sit meditating.

Loha Prasad

A small park nearby with an open pavilion and a **monument to Rama III** presents the ideal opportunity for a rest. On the other side of Maha Chai Road, the restored remains of the **city wall** ⑫ and fort are visible. King Rama I started work on fortifying the city, which in the west was protected by a loop in the Chao Phaya river. The eastern side was secured by a 7-km (4-mile) long, 3.5-m (11-ft) high and 1.8-m (6-ft) wide wall and 15 forts. Chulalongkorn ordered the wall's demolition at the turn of the century and used the rubble as hard core for new roads.

To the south of the bridge over the Khlong Banglampoo boats leave the Phanfa pier and make their way along the stinking sewage canals to the city's eastern suburbs, to Banglampoo and the main station.

Brush barrow

Visible from afar on the other side of the old city boundary stands the **Golden Mount**, which is crowned by the golden *chedi* of **Wat Saket** ⑬. A mound had been created from the earth that was removed when the defensive *khlongs* were constructed and Rama III set about building a giant *chedi* like the one at Ayutthaya at its summit, but the muddy soil gave way and the walls collapsed. Rama V later added more soil and rubble to the Golden Mount and the gilded *chedi* was completed. The viewing hall at an altitude of 78m (255ft) offers a tremendous panorama of the city. In 1897, one of Buddha's bones was interred in the golden *chedi*. It was a present to Chulalongkorn from the viceroy of India, Lord Curzon.

According to legend, in 1782 General Chakri performed the ritual washing ceremony in the Wat Saket at the foot of the hill, after defeating the Cambodians and before his coronation as king. He had the temple built in the traditional style out of gratitude for his victory. The *bot*, with well-preserved murals, is surrounded by open galleries and houses an 18th-century Buddha statue. Some fine teak gates outside the temple grounds open into the *viharn* where a huge, upright Buddha, known as **Phra Attarasa**, is kept. The statue was rescued from the ruins of Sukothai.

The hill is at its most colourful during the Golden Mount Festival in November. Thousands of pilgrims and onlookers make their way up the path to pay their respects to the Buddha relic. The monks of Wat Saket are grateful for the donations and the entertainers and performers also welcome the generosity of visitors.

Climbing the Golden Mount

Route 3

To the home of the king and parliament

The Democracy Memorial – Khaosan Road – Wat Benchamabophit – Vimarnmek Palace

Signs on Khaosan Road

Every evening King Chulalongkorn, the beloved father of modern Thailand, used to drive along the splendid boulevard – built by royal decree – between the Royal Palace and the Throne Hall in the country's first ever limousine. Now, an endless surge of vehicles of every imaginable kind streams along the eight-lane Ratdamnoen Road, so visitors are advised to make a detour to the rear entrance of the Throne Hall.

It is just about possible to complete the first section of this route on foot, but finish the tour by taxi.

Encounters about town

Motorcycle pair

The **Democracy Memorial** in the middle of the round-about on Ratdamnoen Klang Road serves as a reminder of the 1932 *coup d'état*. Fearless pedestrians may wish to cut through the never-ending lines of traffic and look closely at the bas-reliefs that describe the end of 700 years of absolute monarchy and celebrate the birth of the nation's democracy.

The section of road between the Democracy Memorial and the Sanam Luang was the focal point for demonstrations in May 1992. These protests were faced down with what was – for Thailand – great brutality and many demonstrators died or were injured. In the end, however, the military government under prime minister Suchinda was forced to resign and constitutional changes were introduced (*see page 13*).

Behind the grand facades of the administrative and commercial offices in Ratdamnoen Klang Road lies old

Democracy Memorial

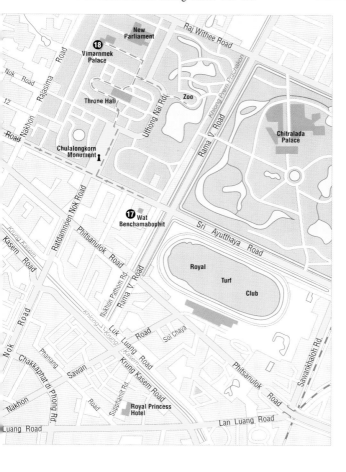

*Khaosan Road
and guesthouses*

Hats galore

Bangkok. Two-storey teak houses with tiny front gardens line the narrow alleys (*sois*) but not even this part of the city is untouched by modernisation. Bulldozers continue to clear space for new office blocks. However, ★ **Khaosan Road** ❶ has undergone the greatest transformation. Since the beginning of the 1980s, this district has been much favoured by backpackers and low-budget tourists. The addresses of the first guesthouses spread quickly by word of mouth and, before long, all available mattresses, even on the balconies, were booked up. This success soon encouraged other guesthouses to spring up and now there are over 100 establishments, not to mention travel agents, cheap restaurants, *bureaux de change*, souvenir stalls and bookshops, all catering for the '20 something' market. Always keep a tight hold of handbags and wallets, as petty criminals and drug addicts regard the area as a good hunting ground.

Some 200m (220yds) further north along the narrow side alleys lies the **Banglampoo textile market**. Many small shops have expanded on to the pavements of Thanom Thani and into the nearby side streets. The sale of fabrics used to be the main attraction for the locals but, more recently, fashionable boutiques have gained a foothold.

Thanom Thani ends in the east at a busy square which is also the terminus for many bus services. Before acceding to the throne, Crown Prince Mongkut lived as a monk and abbot at ★ **Wat Bovornives** ❶ for 27 years. After a thorough study of the Pali scripts, he decided to restore the order to its original function and founded the strict Dhamyutti sect, to which the present-day monks still belong. As an outward symbol of their faith, they wear dark robes and go barefoot. Several princes and kings, including the present King Bhumibol, spent some time here as monks. The *wat* is affiliated to the Maha Mongkut Buddhist University. Reformed, but pure Buddhist teaching is at the heart of the temple's philosophy.

Gilded Chinese carvings surround the entrances to the *bot* and *viharn* – rich Chinese opium dealers hoped that the gods would ignore the shameful nature of their trade. The mouths of the temple-guards at the doors were smeared with pitch so that they could not gossip. Royal crowns on the gables of the T-shaped *bot* refer to Mongkut and confirm the temple's royal connections. Inside (usually locked), the famous **Jinasri Buddha** ('victorious Buddha') stands on a plinth beneath a gilded baldachin, one of the finest works of art from the Sukothai period, or more precisely from 1257 when Sukothai shook off the Khmer yoke. Rama III had the statue brought here from Phitsanulok. Behind it, adopting the same pose in a mystical half-light, stands an even larger gilded Buddha figure, a piece from Phetchaburi. Also of interest are the Chinese-style murals which show how local people perceived the lifestyles of foreigners living in Bangkok during the 19th century. Hidden away in the two *viharn* on either side of the huge, old *bodhi* tree are more Buddha figures. The whole site is dominated by a 50-m (164-ft) high golden *chedi*.

Life in the backstreets

Only 100m (110yds) to the west, at the junction of Phra Sumen Road and Chakrapong Road, cross Khlong Banglampoo, and proceed up Samsen Road for 600m (650 yds) to Wisut Kasat Road. The **Bank of Thailand** on the northwest corner was the epicentre of the July 1997 catastrophe in which Thailand lost US$23 billion while attempting to defend the baht, thereby igniting a financial crisis across Asia. View the bank's fascinating collection of rare coins and enjoy a glass of wine or a meal at **Tang The**, an arty bistro across the street.

The small *sois* in this neighbourhood offer an interesting insight into the daily life of local people of more modest means. Take a walk through any of the narrow alleys to the north of Khlong Banglampoo. It is hard to get lost as the noise of the traffic on the main street is audible all the time. In addition, the *sois* are numbered from south to north (Soi Samsen 2, 4, 6, etc.). Those who cross the *khlong* opposite the Wat Bovornives and head north will join Wisut Kasat Road near the Parliament Hotel.

A path leads from Wisut Kasat Road through a tall, white gateway to the **Wat Indraviharn** (access is also possible from Samsen Road via the Soi 10 Trok Wat In). On the outside wall of the temple, the giant, bright stucco statue, 33m (108ft) high, is particularly eye-catching: a standing Buddha in ochre robes is collecting his morning offerings.

Buddha at Wat Indraviharn

Wat Benchamabophit

Wat Benchamabophit: Buddha and the canal

Wander through the old markets, spread out on both sides of Krung Kasem Road further north. To the east of Samsen Road, household goods, food and fabrics are sold in the covered halls of the **Chanpravit market** and, to the west, on both sides of the *khlong*, the open stalls of the **Thewet market** extend as far as the landing stage for the express river boats. Flowers and plants are the principal offerings on the south bank of the canal, fruit and vegetables on the north bank.

Try a café in the nearby Phitsanulok Road and enjoy a refreshing drink before hailing a taxi for the ★★ **Wat Benchamabophit** , the 'Wat of the Fifth King'. King Chulalongkorn commissioned the so-called 'Marble Temple' in 1899 after his first trip to Europe. It is the last major temple constructed in Bangkok. Designed in a cruciform shape, the exterior is clad in Italian Carrara marble. Stained glass windows depicting angels are a radical departure from traditional window treatments. The cruciform *bot* with its three-tier roof and gleaming golden yellow tiles is visible from afar. Two stone Burmese lions *(singha)* guard the entrance and the interior is decorated with a marble floor and gold murals. The base of the central Buddha, a copy of Phitsanulok's **Phra Buddha Ninnaraj** (which is said to have wept tears of blood when Ayutthaya overran the northern town Sukhothai in the 14th century) contains the ashes of King Chulalongkorn. On three sides, the inner courtyard is overlooked by open galleries, where 53 Buddha images, all roughly the same size (some originals and some copies), are displayed, while a colony of sacred turtles, symbols of a long life, live in the canal.

Early in the morning, the monks can be seen walking through the extensive gardens carrying bowls in which to collect offerings from the faithful.

On the other side of Rama V Road are the grounds of the **Royal Turf Club**. Every Sunday the best racehorses in the country attract thousands of punters and huge sums of money are wagered. The Chinese are dedicated gamblers, but most of the city's casinos have been closed and cockfighting is banned, so the weekly race meetings represent one of the few legal opportunities for betting. Men still gamble on fighting fish, on the winner of a game of *makrut*, a Thai version of chess, and on the outcome of Thai boxing matches.

The **Chitralada Palace**, the permanent residence of the king, is hidden away to the north of the racecourse behind a moat and a high fence. The spacious grounds with fountains, groups of statues and an experimental farm are not open to the public.

From the Marble Temple, follow Sri Ayutthaya Road westward as far as the junction with Ratdamnoen Nok Road. This huge, asphalt square is used for parades, including one held to mark the king's birthday. At the centre stands the **equestrian statue of Rama V**, and to the north the white marble ★ **Throne Hall**. Italian architects, commissioned by Rama V, drew up the plans for this domed, neoclassical structure. When the absolute monarchy was abolished, the parliament met in what used to be the throne room, where the walls and ceilings are covered in scenes depicting historical events. Nowadays, except on special occasions, the deputies meet in the new parliament buildings further north.

The Throne Hall

★★ **Vimarnmek Palace** ⓲ to the northwest of the Throne Hall is definitely worth a visit (guided tours every day, 9.30am–3pm, every 30 minutes; Royal Palace and Wat Phra Kaeo tickets include Vimarnmek Palace). Chulalongkorn had this teak palace built at the beginning of the 20th century. Open galleries and verandahs help to keep the interior cool. The west wing was reserved for the king, his daughters and his concubines, while the north wing was used by the queen and her royal household. During the 1980s, the 80 or so rooms were renovated and about half of them are now open to the public. They contain an astonishing number of valuable antiques and curiosities. The palace is surrounded by several small ponds and classical Thai dance performances are held at 10.30am and 2pm.

Vimarnmek Palace

Bangkok Zoo provides some respite from the stresses and strains of city life. The grounds surround a large lake, that once formed a part of the old palace, and most of the animals are natives of southeast Asia. The rhinos, the large aviary and the orang-utan are special favourites, as are the royal white elephants, the number of which once determined the scale of royal power.

Feeding time at the zoo

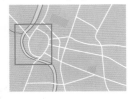

Life by the water

Route 4

The Menam Chao Phaya and the khlongs of Thonburi

Wat Pho – Wat Arun – Thonburi

Rivers and canals, the traditional communication arteries within Thailand, extend from deep into the area surrounding the city. The first local traders and European merchants built their offices, warehouses and dwellings beside these waterways. Colourful markets and splendid temples followed and, more recently, multi-storey blocks comprising offices, owner-occupier flats, hotels and shopping centres have radically altered the skyline. A trip on a hired boat or one of the regular passenger vessels can give a good impression of life by the water's edge, but anyone who wants to see more will have to leave their boat and make their way along the narrow alleys to the many temples and churches that lie off the beaten track.

Hiring a boat is the only way to tour the remote district of Thonburi, where life is a little more simple than in its sister town of Bangkok. Many people live alongside the canals (*khlongs*) in traditional stilted houses and work in the modern offices in the city centre.

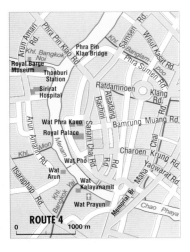

Anyone who does not have enough time to complete the full route should include, at least, the Wat Pho, the 'Temple of the Reclining Buddha', and Wat Arun, the 'Temple of Dawn'. Those wishing to discover a little more, could hire a boat or a taxi and visit Wat Kalayanamit, the Portuguese quarter and the Wat Prayun.

Sixteen gates guarded by giant demons lead through a high wall into ★★ **Wat Pho**, the 'Temple of the Reclining Buddha'. The grand buildings of the largest and oldest *wat* in Bangkok were built in 1789 on the site of a 16th-century temple. Since the reign of Rama III the monastery has been used as a medical school and as a kind of university.

The entrance in **Chetuphon Road** leads into the eastern temple area which contains the main shrine. This is overlooked by long galleries housing 394 magnificent, gilded Buddhas in various styles. The main Buddha figures from the Sukhothai and Ayutthaya periods are located in the four *viharn* set in the galleries, one for each side. The ★ **bot**, one of the finest in Bangkok, stands on a marble plinth with bas-reliefs depicting scenes from the *Ramayana*. Pull the stone ball from the mouth of a Chinese stone lion without breaking the ball or the mouth and you are guaranteed eternal life.

Images of Wat Pho

Chedis of varying sizes are situated in the courtyard and there is a *viharn* at each corner. On the eastern side of the courtyard is the **School of Traditional Massage**, where you can enjoy a relaxing massage or receive tuition in the skills of this traditional therapy. Murals and statues in the temple area illustrate the various techniques. Traditional Thai massage has nothing to do with the services offered in the gloomy salons of Patpong Road. The real thing is based on reflex massages, yoga and acupuncture. It originated from the 1,000-year-old Indian therapies which came to Thailand with Buddhism. Strong thumbs dig deep into tense muscles and work away at the body's energy points. Fingers are stretched until the joints crack and the masseurs bring their full body weight to bear as they rub vigorously up and down on either side of the spinal column. When the

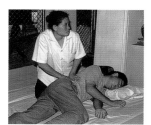

Traditional massage

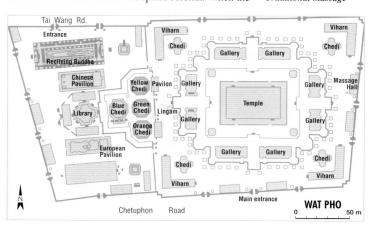

WAT PHO

0   50 m

pressure from hands, feet and elbows ceases, the pain gives way to a pleasant feeling of relief. The energy balance is restored, the muscles relax, swellings fade away and pain is relieved. At the end of a one- or two-hour session, both body and soul are refreshed.

The path into the western area passes a *lingam*, decorated with colourful fabrics, which is a symbol of fertility. In a small pavilion, murals with medical themes serve as a reminder that the principles of eastern medicine were passed on here. Four large *chedis* covered with porcelain decorations were built by the first Chakri kings. The green one with its standing Buddha is attributed to Rama I, the yellow and orange ones to Rama III and the blue one to Rama IV. The **library** is also richly decorated with porcelain ornaments. Just to the south behind a pond is the **Europeans' Pavilion**, and to the north, around a tree, the **Chinese Pavilion**.

Reclining Buddha's feet

36

Many tour groups are taken directly to the *viharn* of the ★★ **Reclining Buddha**. This impressive statue, which is covered entirely with gold, measures 45m (147ft) long and 15m (50ft) tall. It was built by Rama III and illustrates the passing of Buddha into *nirvana*. One hundred and eight mother-of-pearl ornaments in the soles of its feet represent the characteristics of a Buddha. As the statue is protected by bars, the faithful make their gold leaf offerings to replica figures.

The dwellings and lecture-halls for the 300 or so monks are located to the south of Chetuphon Road.

From the gate in **Tai Wang Road**, it is only a few yards back to Thien Pier where the express boats, *khlong* boats and ferries to Thonburi moor. Take a ferry across to one of Thailand's grandest sacred buildings, ★★ **Wat Arun**, the Temple of Dawn. In the Ayutthaya period the *prang*

Aspects of Wat Arun

was just 15 metres (50ft) high; today the 67-m (220-ft) high *prang*, completed during the reign of Rama III, is broken up into terraces, which are partly accessible by steep steps. It is worth the climb to the highest terrace for the magnificent view across the river and the old town as far as the multi-storey blocks in the Silom Road area.

The tall, tapering central *prang* is surrounded by four smaller ones. These towers symbolise the Buddhist universe with the sacred Mount Meru at the centre. All the outer walls are decorated with stucco, glass, pastel faience, colourful Chinese porcelain and earthenware fragments. Set into the niches are figures of the god Indra on the three-headed elephant Erawan and the god of wind Phra Pai on his white stallion. The *bot* to the north of the *prang* contains the ashes of Rama II. Like many Chinese statues in Bangkok, those in the inner courtyard arrived here as ships' ballast from China.

Wat Arun: the inner courtyard

Most of the boats which sail upstream from here will pass the Royal Barges, after the **Sirirat Hospital** (on the Thonburi side), which was founded by the present king's father, who was also a doctor. Behind it railway lines converge on **Thonburi station** (Bangkok Noi station). Before any bridges were built over the river, the trains to Hua Hin and the other southern cities left from here. Now Thonburi station is used only by a few trains for the River Kwai region and further south.

The boat now enters the Khlong Bangkok Noi which links Bangkok with Nonthaburi in the west. The ★ **Royal Barge Museum** is situated on the north bank opposite Thonburi station (daily 8.30am–4.30pm; no photographs). A number of vessels restored for the city's bicenntenial anniversary are stored in sheds here. They were formerly used during the Tot Kathin Festival at the end of October when the king travelled downstream to Wat Arun to hand over new robes and temple instruments to the monks. He would sit under a canopy on the **Sri Supana Hong**, whose prow resembles the mythical swan of the same name. For the last procession, **Anantanakaraj**, with its majestic seven-headed *naga* serpent, bore a sacred Buddha figure. **Aneakchat Bhuchong**, the third vessel, can be identified by its *garuda* birds. The barges were used in 1996 when the king became the world's longest reigning monarch, and again on his 72nd birthday in 1999.

Royal Barge Museum

Take a taxi or a hired boat south to the old Portuguese quarter. The tall roof of the *viharn* in the **Wat Kalayanamit** (Wat Kalaya) to the south of the Khlong Bangkok Yai is visible from afar. During the Chinese New Year festivals, devout Buddhists bring huge seated Buddha statues as offerings, give thanks to Buddha and pray for guidance. The monastery here was founded by Rama III

Wat Kalayanamit

and the columns and walls in the interior are painted in Chinese style, while the bell in the courtyard is said to be the biggest in the country.

Santa Cruz Church

Tiny alleys and waterways criss-cross the district between Khlong Bangkok Yai and Prachathipok Road. **Santa Cruz Church**, once the focal point for the Portuguese quarter, lies a good 10-minute walk away. The first European merchants to settle in Bangkok during the 16th century were Portuguese, and the church, which was rebuilt at the beginning of the 20th century, is now the lively centre of the Catholic community. Mass is held here every morning and jasmine garlands are left by a grotto near the church.

The **Wat Prayun** (Prayunrawongsawad) monastery, with its remarkable wooden carvings on the gables of the *bot* and *viharn* and fine mother-of-pearl inlays in the doors, is often used for funerals. An unusual feature is the cemetery: on a bizarrely-shaped rock surrounded by an artificial lake, memorial tablets, small *chedis*, Buddhist temples, Christian churches and other buildings have been constructed in honour of the dead. Many turtles, symbols of longevity, live in the temple grounds and visitors often feed them with fruit.

The Memorial Bridge

The **Memorial Bridge** (1932), the first river crossing to link Thonburi with the Chinese quarter, honours Rama I. When this bridge proved unable to cope with the volume of traffic, the Phra Pokklao Bridge was built parallel to it. From the middle of the new span there is an excellent view downriver; the old span provides views of Wat Arun and the boats upriver. Many inhabitants like to make offerings at the monument to the city's founder.

To return to the city centre, take a taxi or an express boat from the Saphan Phut pier by the Pak Khlong Talaad market. Otherwise, hire a boat for a tour of the *khlongs*.

Braving the Chao Phaya

Through the khlongs of Thonburi

Seven bridges, countless ferries and express boats connect Bangkok with Thonburi, its counterpart on the other side of the Menam Chao Phaya. During the rush hour, however, the boats and bridges can scarcely cope with the sheer volume of traffic. Until fairly recently the river presented an almost insuperable barrier protecting Thonburi from the effects of modernisation in Bangkok, and to the west of the Menam Chao Phaya, life continued at a relaxed pace. But time has finally caught up with Thonburi, and many canals were filled in and replaced with busy highways. Many idyllic spots by the *khlongs* have had to make way for the new roads and housing estates, and it is now necessary to go some way out to find the old atmosphere of the time when the only way of getting between the stilted houses was by boat.

The dwellings that face the *khlongs* can only be reached from small jetties with covered pavilions. Coconut palms and mango trees grow right up to the water's edge, men and women bathe in their shadow and children splash around noisily. Floating supermarkets and food stalls keep the people supplied with fresh fare.

Various travel agents organise trips to the floating market near Wat Sai, which is actually less interesting than the market in Damnoen Saduak (*see page 55*). The Wat Sai market, where some 30 or so boats paddle up and down and Thai girls in straw hats try to tempt onlookers into buying oranges, bananas, water-melons, pineapples and other tropical fruit, is only maintained for the tourists. Most visitors book a boat trip from the Oriental Hotel pier, but a much more interesting way of exploring the *khlongs* is to hire a *hang yao* along the Khlong Bangkok Yai and Khlong Sanam Chai from the pier near the Memorial Bridge. These narrow, manoeuvrable boats are the main form of transport and a scheduled service runs along the *khlongs*. A ride costs only a few baht and the boat will stop at any jetty if requested. When the water levels are high during the rainy season, boat transport is halted on some canals on account of the low bridges; during the dry season low water levels also bring some services to a standstill.

Exploring the khlongs

Hang yao can be privately chartered at several piers. Pay when boarding and sit on the low boards as close as possible to the front. At the rear there is a greater risk of being splashed. An umbrella can be useful in this respect – and will also function as a parasol. Give a nod to the driver and he will stop at the next jetty.

Take care when using the regular boat services in the late afternoon. Many of the boat owners who live by the *khlongs* are likely to head for home after 5pm and travellers can be left stranded miles from their hotel. A taxi will be the only way of returning to the city centre.

Chinatown

Route 5

The Chinese and Indian quarters

Hua Lamphong station – the Golden Buddha – Yaowarat Road – Sampeng Lane – Pahurat Road

A wander through Bangkok's most densely populated district might may prove a test of nerves for some people. Surrounded by traffic, the industrious Chinese will be selling, cooking and eating, oblivious to the overwhelming din and pollution-laden air. If you don't want to walk the whole route, cover the longer stretches by taxi.

The tour begins by the **Hua Lamphong main station**, where trains leave to almost all parts of the country. The tall roof was built in 1890 and was modelled on one of Manchester's main-line terminals in the UK. The first line went as far as Nakhon Ratchasima (*Khorat*), and 30 years later it was extended to Chiang Mai and Singapore.

Wat Traimit: Golden Buddha

It is not far from here to the **Wat Traimit ⑲**. In a two-storey structure at the 'Temple of the Three Friends' stands the famous ★★**Golden Buddha**. This masterpiece from the Sukhotai period is 3.5m (11ft) high, weighs 5.5 tons and is 80 percent gold. It was discovered when the port was expanded, covered with a thick layer of plaster. The plaster-coated statue was initially brought to Wat Traimit and kept beneath a temporary roof until a permanent home was found. When the statue was being moved, it fell over and had to be left overnight in the rain. The next day, the gold could be seen shining through the plaster. This layer of camouflage had probably been applied over 300 years earlier when the Burmese invaders destroyed Ayutthaya.

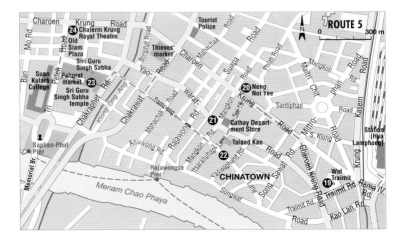

To reach Chinatown from here, take a taxi along Charoen Krung Road, formerly New Road, in a north-east direction. Start your tour of the district with a visit to a Chinese temple: the **Neng Noi Yee** ⑳ (on the corner of Charoen Krung Road and Mangkon Road; the Thais call it Wat Mangkon Malawat). A number of Chinese gods stand on the altars, alongside the Buddha statues and these are the objects of veneration on Chinese holidays.

Neng Noi Yee temple

The main thoroughfare in Chinatown is the narrow and noisy **Yaowarat Road** ㉑, which runs parallel to Charoen Krung Road. In the Chinese chemists, look out for exotic roots and fruits, dried lizards and sea-horses, bones and horns, whose medicinal qualities are released when they are ground down to a powder.

Chinese chemist

On the other side of the large Cathay Department Store, Itsaranuhap Lane branches off Yaowarat Road. This is the site of the **Talaad Kao market**. Among the more mundane produce, look out for the mountains of fish crackers and sacks of dried fish and shrimps.

Just beyond is the narrow ★ **Sampeng Lane** ㉒ (Soi Wanit 1). Take the opportunity here to browse through fabrics, household goods, the useful and the useless. Some of the shops sell religious items such as incense sticks, paper money, statues of deities, everything that a believer needs for family festivals, temple ceremonies and daily ancestor worship. On weekdays, it can be a struggle to get past the throngs of people, hand-carts and motorbikes, not to mention the goods themselves.

A detour north along the Chakrawat Road takes in the **Thieves' Market** (Nakhon Kasem). The name for this market between Charoen Krung Road, Yaowarat Road, Chakrawat Road and the canal is rather misleading as most of the traders sell perfectly legal brassware, machine parts, musical instruments, furniture and some antiques.

Much more interesting, however, is the Indian **Pahurat market** on the other side of Chakrawat Road. Here stalls overflow with materials, clothes, linen and haberdashery. Soaring above the market place are the golden domes of the Sikh **Sri Guru Singh Sabha temple** ㉓.

Old Siam Plaza, on the other side of Pahurat Road, is a modern shopping centre that contrasts sharply with the traditional market. Beneath the restored glass-roofed halls of an old market, small retail shops sell mainly materials and porcelain. Local specialities are sold in the food market and there are several restaurants and a pleasant café. During the 1930s one of the most modern theatres in Asia was opened by the king in the northwest section of the shopping centre. After lavish restoration work, the **Chalerm Krung Royal Theatre** ㉔ has now re-opened and is the gleaming new venue for performances of the classical Ramayana dance theatre.

Royal Theatre

The modern cityscape

Route 6

The European-style quarters of Bangrak and Sathorn

Charoen Krung Road – the Oriental Hotel – Silom Road

This tour explores the city's more recent past, a turbulent period in which Bangkok has been transformed into a pulsating metropolis. Multi-storey office blocks dominate the landscape and it is easy to miss the historic buildings – old colonial-style country houses, markets and offices. It is worth taking a look round this part of the city at night when a quite different side is on view. Many of the restaurants offer a wide selection of specialities.

One of Bangkok's busiest streets, **Charoen Krung Road** (also known as New Road), runs parallel to the river from Wat Pho southward through Chinatown. In 1861 Rama IV planned the construction of Bangkok's first road. Many European businessmen were complaining that there were too few opportunities for riding and taking fresh air and that their enjoyment was limited by the lack of bridges over the canals. Temporary bridges were built and these lasted for 30 years before Chulalongkorn called on a team of Italian engineers to provide something more permanent. In 1883 he introduced a European-style postal system, fol-

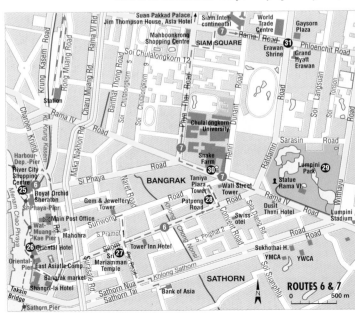

The terrace of the Oriental Hotel

43

lowed a few years later by a telephone system (a monument outside the General Post Office recalls the early days of these services). The grand, European-style post and telegraph buildings still fulfil their original functions. A walk along the narrow lanes between the river and Charoen Krung Road will provide an interesting insight into life in Bangkok.

By the Si Phaya pier where the Khlong Krung Kasem flows into the Menam Chao Phaya stand the **River City Shopping Centre** and the **Royal Orchid Sheraton Hotel**; many of the restaurant boats moor here in the evenings (*see page 74*). Just to the south of the pier, the Portuguese Embassy and lush gardens hidden behind tall walls remind tourists of a time when merchants' villas and foreign embassies overlooked the river.

Now leave the traffic behind and take to the river, if only for a short journey. It is just two stops to the **Oriental Hotel**, one of the best hotels in the world. The old wing, where many famous guests have stayed, retains some of its old charm. If time and money permit, enjoy a cocktail on the riverside terrace and watch the boats pass by.

The whitewashed building just south of the landing stage was built for the Danish **East Asiatic Company** at around the turn of the century. Behind it rises the tower of the Catholic **Assumption Cathedral**, where an English-language service is held every Sunday at 10am. One impressive aspect of the English colonial-style seat of the Bishop of Bangkok is the contrasting use of white and brown stone. The nearby college is regarded as one of the country's top schools.

Early in the morning, behind the **Shangri-La Hotel** and just before the Taksin Bridge (also known as the Sathorn Bridge), the **Bangrak market** is a hive of activity: housewives and cooks from the nearby restaurants will be on

East Asiatic Company
Assumption Cathedral

Sri Mariamman Temple

Night lights in Patpong
Elevated train over Ratdamri Road

the look-out for fresh vegetables, fruit, meat and seafood. Other commodities on sale include a wide choice of orchids, plus other flowers and fabrics.

The Hindu **Sri Mariamman Temple** ㉗ stands beside Silom Road (on the corner of Pan Road), its tall gatetower *(gopuram)* typical of temples in southern India. The temple is used as a starting-point for processions to mark the main Hindu celebrations such as the Thaipusam festival at the end of January/beginning of February.

The narrow strip of road between the river and Charoen Krung Road was built in the last hundred years. Only isolated farmhouses stood along the four parallel *khlongs* that flowed into the river. These waterways have been filled in and replaced by the wide **Si Phaya Road**, **Suriwong Road** and **Silom Road**, which are lined by hotels, restaurants and shops. Further south, **Sathorn Nua Road** and **Sathorn Tai Road** on either side of the Sathorn Khlong cut through the diplomatic quarter. Land prices have reached astronomical proportions here and many of the delightful villas set in tropical gardens have had to make way for multi-storey office blocks. One of the most unusual is the 'Robot Building' belonging to the **Bank of Asia**, which was designed by the famous architect Dr Sumet Jumsai and completed in 1986. The blue-glass **Gem and Jewellery Tower** in Suriwong Road, an important exchange in the world gem market, is one of the district's newest structures. Graeco-Roman influences are evident in the architecture of the **Wall Street Tower**, 33 Suriwong Road and the **Taniya Plaza Tower** near Patpong Road. Look carefully and you will see spirit houses on the roofs of the modern glass and marble buildings.

The notorious **Patpong Road** ㉘ *(see page 78)* runs between Silom and Suriwong Road. The **night market** stalls open up about 4pm.

Route 7

The eastern highlights

Lumpini Park – Sukhumvit Road – Jim Thompson House – Suan Pakkad Palace

Bangkok spreads out eastward along the main traffic thoroughfares, Sri Ayutthaya Road, Petchburi Road, Rama I Road and Rama IV Road. One or two green spaces offer some respite from the din of the heavy traffic, but they are increasingly under threat from the relentless demand for flats, office blocks and hotel complexes. Anyone wanting to miss out on the experience of a Bangkok traffic jam should undertake this tour on a Sunday. During the week, avoid the rush hour (6.30–9am and 3.30–6pm).

Lumpini Park

Lumpini Park ㉙ is a must for all visitors to Bangkok. To make the most of it, get up early, even before dawn, and watch the joggers, bodybuilders and old men practising *tai chi* (shadow boxing). Later on, explore the lake by pedalo and during the dragon-flying season (from February to April) watch whole families testing out their paper kites. A statue of Rama I marks the entrance to the park and there is also a good Chinese restaurant.

45

The Pasteur Institute runs a ★ **Snake Farm ㉚** on Rama IV Road (Monday to Friday, 8.30am–4.30pm, Saturday, Sunday and holidays, 8.30am–noon). Its main aim in breeding the snakes is to obtain anti-venom serum to counter Thailand's many poisonous species. The reptiles are 'milked' of their venom at around 10.30am and 2pm. Dare-devils can be photographed in the embrace of a python and other less dangerous species.

A venomous display

Just over a kilometre north of here is parallel **Rama I Road**, the main east–west axis, which going east becomes **Ploenchit Road** and then **Sukhumvit Road**. Many international hotels are located beside this busy road, providing customers for the restaurants, huge shopping centres and bars. The section of Rama I Road around the Siam Intercontinental Hotel, Siam Square and the Siam Centre is the oldest of Bangkok's shopping quarters. Many of the shops sell materials and jewellery, but there are also cinemas and Western fast-food restaurants. In contrast to the gleaming shopping precincts, the stalls in the maze of streets around **Siam Square** look distinctly old-fashioned. The **Mahboonkrong Shopping Centre** on Phya Thai Road is the most popular meeting spot for Thais.

Bangkok's new elevated railway will make possible an aerial view of **Wat Pathumwanara**, previously hidden behind high walls on Rama I Road near the World Trade Centre. It is a haven of peace containing murals of

Opposite: devotees at the Erawan Shrine
Below: Erawan shrine dancer

Jim Thompson House: Ayutthayan carving

Suan Pakkad

Sithanonchai, a hero of Thai literature, and with a small, neat temple garden.

The Hindu ★ **Erawan Shrine** ㉛, near the Grand Hyatt Erawan Hotel, is always a busy spot. The faithful arrive at all times of day to offer incense sticks, jasmine garlands and carved elephants to a statue of the four-faced god Brahma. Special credit is given to those who pay dancers to perform for the deity. The splendid spirit house, formerly in the Erawan Hotel, was built in the 1950s when, after a number of mishaps, it was thought that the spirits needed placating. The hotel was demolished in 1988. Brahma is thought to be particularly helpful on money matters and lottery draws attract many worshippers.

Across Ploenchit Road stands the elegant, new **Gaysorn Plaza**, filled with upmarket European boutiques and restaurants, while diagonally opposite the shrine is the **World Trade Centre**, comprising a large department store, restaurants, funfairs, tennis courts and, on the seventh floor, an ice-rink. Other shopping centres, such as the **Peninsula Plaza** the **Central Department Store**, Bangkok's oldest, are within easy reach of this junction.

Those interested in seeing a fabulous collection of antiques should take a taxi to the ★★ **Jim Thompson House** (Monday to Saturday, 9am–4pm). Jim Thompson came to Bangkok as an American intelligence officer after World War II and set about building up the country's silk industry. He introduced new techniques and silkworms that produced higher yields. Materials that had up until then been sold exclusively to the home market were improved with new colours and designs and sold for export. Thompson became rich, bought six teak houses over 100 years old and combined them to make an estate. As a lover of Thai art, he filled his home with valuable pieces. The interior of the house which was transported here from Ayutthaya is much admired for its unique collection of handicrafts and priceless antiques from all over southeast Asia and these can be viewed as part of a guided tour. Thompson mysteriously disappeared while walking in Malaysia's Cameron Highlands.

It may be a good idea to take a taxi to the ★ **Suan Pakkad Palace** on Sri Ayutthaya Road a little further north (Monday to Saturday, 9am–4pm). Within the spacious gardens, five traditional Thai palace-style houses have been erected and decorated with household goods and antiques: furniture, bronzes, statues from the Dvaravati and Khmer periods, porcelain, Ban Chiang pottery, musical instruments, weapons, etc. Perhaps the finest exhibit is a pavilion in the garden, that, after thorough restoration, was brought here from Bang Pa by Princess Chumbot. It is a unique example of Siamese art from the Ayutthaya period.

Dwellings on the Chao Phaya

Excursion boat

Excursion 1

North to Ayutthaya

The Shrine of the Storks – Bang Pa In – Ayutthaya – Khao Yai National Park

A trip to the former royal city of Ayutthaya is a must for anyone with an interest in Thai culture. Other attractions include the 'Shrine of the Storks', recommended for bird-watchers, and the large craft centre at Bang Sai. A day trip to Ayutthaya is feasible, but it is better to stay the night. Even though it is a three-hour car ride from the capital, an excursion to the Khao Yai National Park is also worthwhile. Here too an overnight stop is recommended.

If just one day is available, then take a trip on the river. It will give a fascinating insight into everyday life on the banks of the Menam Chao Phaya. Every morning at about

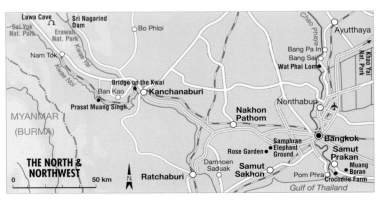

8am, luxury boats set sail from the River City Shopping Complex, Royal Orchid Sheraton and Oriental Hotel for Bang Pa In and Ayutthaya. Every Sunday at about 8am, an express boat leaves Chang pier for Bang Pa In via Wat Phai Lom and Bang Sai (two-hour journey), returning in the afternoon (for further information, tel: 222 53 30).

Ornithologists in particular will enjoy the first stop. Thousands of open-billed storks nest in the woods around the **Wat Phai Lom**, the 'Shrine of the Storks'. The birds build their nests in November and December; they breed and then, in April and May, return with their young to the swamps of Bangladesh.

Queen Sirikit provided the impetus for the **Royal Folk Arts and Crafts Centre** (Tuesday to Saturday, 9am–4pm) on the banks of the Chao Phaya near **Bang Sai**. At the centre, young people from all parts of Thailand are trained in traditional crafts by the country's most experienced artisans. Visitors are free to watch the production of fabrics, wickerwork, furniture and glassware, which later go on sale in the adjoining shop, in the Chitralada Handicraft Shops in Bangkok's Royal Palace and at the international airport.

Arts and crafts near Bang Sai

★★ Bang Pa In

The summer residence of the Ayutthaya kings which stands on an island in the river was built in the 17th century by King Prasat Thong, but it was abandoned 150 years later when the capital was moved to Thonburi. Once steam-powered ships became available to King Mongkut, reconstruction of the palaces at Ayutthaya began. Mongkut's son, Chulalongkorn, continued the work and spent every summer at Bang Pa In.

The classical Thai-style ★★ **Water Pavilion**, which is set in the middle of a lake, is the main attraction. The slender columns bear a three-tier roof, which is crowned by a Siamese tower. Beneath it stands a bronze statue of King Chulalongkorn wearing a field marshal's uniform.

Warophat Phiman served as the king's residence and throne hall. The gleaming red ★ **Wehart Chamrun**, a gift from the Chinese community, is located in a well-tended park. Some exquisite porcelain and furniture, lavishly decorated with gilded carvings and lacquered and mother-of-pearl inlay work, can be seen in the large, two-storey palace. **Uthayan Phumisathian**, a green-painted wooden house in the style of an alpine chalet, was Chulalongkorn's favourite residence.

Chulalongkorn enjoyed studying the stars and he often retreated to his observatory, a round tower on an island in the lake. An obelisk here recalls the memory of Chulalongkorn's principal wife, Queen Sunantha. She and her three children were all drowned in a boating accident.

Ayutthaya, the old capital

★★ *Ayutthaya*

King U Thong founded Ayutthaya in 1350 and the city remained the capital of the Siamese empire until 1767. During the 16th century, it was the economic and cultural focus of southeast Asia and was said to have had more inhabitants than Paris. Within its walls lived merchants and artisans from all over the world. In its heyday many splendid temples and palaces were built, but these all fell victim to the destructive Burmese conquerors. A festival every December commemorates Ayutthaya's golden years.

Situated within a loop in the Chao Phaya and its tributaries, the Lopburi and Pa Sak, the ruined town covers a huge area 5km (3 miles) by 3km (2 miles). Before it was destroyed, it was exposed to attacks from the Burmese army, so a city wall and other fortifications were built.

Some valuable finds from the surrounding area are displayed in the fascinating ★ **Chao Sam Praya National Museum** (Wednesday to Sunday, 9am–noon and 1–4pm). Exhibits date mainly from the Lopburi, U Thong and Ayutthaya periods, although there are a number of exquisite sculptures in Sukothai and Dvaravati style. The museum's showpieces include a giant Buddha head from the 15th century, which stands near the entrance, and the treasury on the first floor.

The ★★ **Ayutthaya Historical Study Centre** is set in a modern building about 300m (330yds) to the east of the old museum (Wednesday to Sunday, 9am–4pm except public holidays). Display boards, dioramas, illustrations and models of ships, temples and dwellings show how the people lived and explore Ayutthaya's role as a capital, as a trading centre and as an administrative centre.

Highlights of the site itself include the remains of the former **Royal Palace** (Wang Luang), which was destroyed right down to its foundations. ★ **Wat Sri Sanphet**, the

Buddha at Wat Sri Sanphet

royal temple just to the south, was built in the 15th century. It housed the 16-m (52-ft) high gilded Buddha statue **Phra Sri Sanphet**. The Burmese burnt down the temple to obtain the gold. Resting beneath the tall roof of the adjacent **Viharn Phra Mongkol Bophit** is Thailand's largest seated Buddha. ★ **Phra Mongkol Bophit** was cast in bronze around 1615 but was badly damaged during the Burmese invasion. Much revered by pilgrims, this Buddha was restored in 1958 and kept in the rebuilt *viharn*. It was gilded in 1992 to commemorate the king's 60th birthday. To the west of the Royal Palace, just a little to one side, the Wat Lokaya Sutha hides beneath palm trees. Between what is left of two ornamented *chedis* and the foundations of pillars that supported the roof of the *bot* lies the well-preserved 28-m (92-ft) long figure of a ★ **Reclining Buddha**.

Wat Phra Ram dates from 1369. It was built as a burial site for the first, U Thong kings, and its tall *prang* dominates the ruins, which are grouped around a stone terrace with *chedis*, Buddha statues, *garudas* and *nagas*.

Wat Phra Ram

At the heart of the old city on the other side of Rama Park, the ruins of the ★ **Wat Mahathat** rise up. This temple is said to have been founded in 1374 under King Ramesuan. Several buildings were grouped around a 44-m (145-ft) high *prang*, which has partially collapsed. The large stone Buddha image in front of the *prang* looks particularly attractive in the twilight.

51

★ *Khao Yai National Park*

Thailand's first national park was opened in 1962 around the 1,352-m (4,434-ft) high Khao Laem. By then, it was really too late as much of the mountain jungle had been burnt down by new settlers. However, the remaining woodland became a sanctuary for one of the country's largest elephant herds. Many other species have also found a refuge here and a small exhibition in the park's headquarters documents how the wildlife has prospered. During the first few years of the park's existence, little was done to protect the natural environment. A golf course was built behind the headquarters and hundreds of tourists stayed in the adjoining bungalow complex. It was not until 1992 that the authorities started to take nature conservation seriously and all the tourist facilities were closed. It is still possible to follow elephant trails along waymarked footpaths and some of the waterfalls may be visited without guides. Permission for longer hikes on the more remote paths must be obtained from the park staff who may, if necessary, supply a guide. Visitors wishing to observe the animals will probably be told to join one of the night tours which local hotels organise. Cars with powerful searchlights are used to pick out the wildlife.

A deer forages for food

One of the park's many waterfalls

Excursion 2

Northwest to Kanchanaburi and the River Kwai

A day trip by rail from Thonburi to Kanchanaburi via Nakhon Pathom, and then along the River Kwai as far as Nam Tok, can be booked as an organised tour or can be undertaken independently. Trains leave from Thonburi station and buses from the Southern Bus Terminal. To include the national park and the historic sites near Kanchanaburi allow at least another two days.

A bus trip to Nakhon Pathom can be interrupted at the **Rose Garden and Country Resort** (32km/20 miles) west of Bangkok. Despite the swimming pools, restaurants, golf course and bungalow accommodation, it is the Thailand Show that attracts most visitors. Starting at about 1.30pm every day in the Cultural Village, this two-hour tour through Thai culture is ideal for tourists in a hurry. Events include working elephants, artisans, traditional wedding ceremonies, the ordination of monks, folk dancing, Siamese music and traditional sports such as Thai boxing.

52

Traditional bamboo dance

Destined for the souvenir shops

Samphran Elephant Ground and Zoo is just a few yards away from the Rose Garden. Its crocodiles have a dual role: three times a day (12.45, 2.20 and 4.30pm), they perform for the visitors; elsewhere, souvenir shops sell handbags and other gift items made from their skin. The elephants also entertain the crowds in the afternoon (1.45 and 3.30pm).

Nakhon Pathom

Mariners are said to have spread Buddhist teaching along the coast around 100BC. Nakhon Pathom lay by the sea and was the capital of the Nakhon Chaisi Mon empire. Around the end of the first millennium, Khmer tribes invaded and the original *chedi*, which contained a relic of the Buddha, was replaced with a Cambodian *prang*. The latter fell into disrepair when the Khmer withdrew, but during the reign of King Mongkut work started on building a Sinhalese *chedi* over the ruined *prang*, and the ancient relic is now hidden away under the ★★ **Phra Pathom Chedi**, which is generally regarded as the oldest Buddhist shrine in Thailand. This huge tower, which is covered with gleaming gold faience tiles, has a diameter of 98m (321ft) and reaches a height of 128m (420ft). It is one of the highest Buddhist monuments in the world (higher than the Shwedagon Pagoda in Rangoon).

A small museum (Wednesday to Sunday, 9am–noon and 1–4pm) to the south of the *chedi* displays finds from the Dvaravati period, Buddha heads and a stone 'wheel of the teachings', which is said to date from 150BC.

Kanchanaburi

Rice fields, sugar cane plantations and tall sugar palms line the route from Nakhon Pathom to Kanchanaburi. This provincial capital, some 130km (80 miles) northwest of Bangkok, is situated on the left bank of the Maekhlong river, which starts here at the confluence of the Kwae Yai and Kwae Noi (Great and Little Kwae). At a number of jetties, boats offer tours along both rivers and through the town. Floating restaurants and discos on the extensive waterway network are also very popular.

Visitor at the JEATH museum

The area is famous throughout the world for the film *Bridge over the River Kwai*, which recalls events here during World War II (*see below*). A number of places in the town remember the many victims of the war. In the Wat Chai Chumphon, the JEATH War Museum (JEATH: Japan, England, Australia, Thailand, Holland) has a reconstruction of the prisoner-of-war huts. On the bamboo walls above the long bunk beds hang letters, photos and other documents which detail the suffering of the 62,000 Allied soldiers and 200,000 forced labour conscripts from Thailand, Burma, India, China, Indonesia and Malaya, many of whom died of cholera, starvation, fever and malaria. Almost 7,000 prisoners-of-war are buried in the two cemeteries 300m (330yds) south of the station and 3km (2 miles) southwest of the town near Kao Pun.

Cemetery

Take a train or a *songtaew* (minibus) from Kanchanaburi to get to the Kwai Bridge, which is to the northwest of the town. The **World War II Museum** just south of the bridge has an unusual collection of exhibits, ranging from Stone Age tools to life-size statues of historical figures including Churchill, Hitler and Einstein.

The story of the bridge

On 8 December 1941, the Japanese army invaded Thailand. After some initial resistance, the military govern-

The Kwai bridge today

ment under General Pibul Songkhram agreed to a cease-fire, thus enabling the Japanese to attack and conquer Malaya and Singapore. The opponents of the military alliance formed themselves into a resistance group, calling themselves the Seri Thai, and they received support from Allied agents. This was the background for Pierre Boulle's novel, *The Bridge over the River Kwai*.

In June 1942, Allied prisoners-of-war and conscripted workers from Thailand and neighbouring countries started work on a 415-km (257-mile) long railway line from Bang Pong to the Three Pagoda Pass separating Thailand from Burma. The Japanese wanted to be able to supply their troops in the event of an attack on India and also be able to impose a naval blockade. Originally, the workers built a wooden bridge a short distance downstream from the present crossing, but this was replaced by a steel construction during the war. It was damaged by American bombers in February 1945.

Day trips from Kanchanaburi

Saluting the fallen
The 'Death Railway'

The 'Death Railway' still runs from Kanchanaburi as far as Nam Tok, along the same track that was laid by prisoners-of-war and conscripted labourers, who worked in extremely difficult terrain, often in malaria-infested swamps. Some sections through the Three Pagoda Pass into Burma were dismantled by the Allies after the war. All that remains is the single-track line to Nam Tok – now something of a tourist attraction. Certainly, the journey across the **River Kwai Bridge**, 4km (2½ miles) north-west of Kanchanaburi, and the breathtaking 500m (550yd) long ★ **Wang Po Viaduct**, high above the Kwae Noi just outside Nam Tok, make for an exhilarating experience.

Tha Kilen station lies just under an hour away from the famous bridge and the village of **Ban Kao** is a further 6km (4 miles) along Highway 3228. An archaeologist working on the railway as a prisoner-of-war was among the first to discover the Neolithic site here. More excavation work at the beginning of the 1960s unearthed burial sites where fully preserved skeletons, votive offerings and the remains of settlements from the Early Stone Age were found. Various exhibits can be seen in the Ban Kao National Museum (Wednesday to Sunday, 9am–4pm) by the river, 2km (1¼ miles) west of the village.

The ★ **Erawan National Park**, 65km (40 miles) north-west of Kanchanaburi by the upper reaches of the Kwae Yai, has become one of the country's most popular parks, mainly thanks to the waterfalls that splash down through a pleasantly cool, wooded valley. The mountain streams trickle down from basin to basin in seven stages. At the weekends, locals climb up to the first stage to picnic and to enjoy swimming in the refreshing water.

Excursion 3

South of Bangkok

Damnoen Saduak – Ratchaburi – Phetchaburi –Kaeng Krachan National Park – Hua Hin

Anyone who enjoys photography should visit the floating market of Damnoen Saduak. Given their proximity to Bangkok and the good transport facilities, the resorts of Hua Hin and Cha-am are popular with locals and tourists alike. They offer good opportunities for rest and relaxation and have hotels of all categories.

★ Damnoen Saduak (110km/68 miles). One of the last floating markets trades on the canals in this small town west of Bangkok. Before dawn, traders arrive with fresh fruit and vegetables from nearby fields. Manoeuvring their little boats skilfully on the crowded waters, they cook, sell and exchange produce on the water. But this is not authentic country life, as tourists come in droves and there are many souvenir shops. Tours from Bangkok often include a trip along the coast or a visit to the Rose Garden. Independent travellers catch the 6am bus from Bangkok's Southern Bus Terminal. From the terminus, take a minibus, a scheduled boat, or a river taxi to the market. At **★ Samut Songkhram** (98km/60 miles), birthplace of the Siamese Twins Eng and Chang (you can visit their statue), the Cathedral of the Virgin Mary and the Rama II Park are popular destinations. Agro-tourism (through the Ministry of Agriculture) offers visits to local fruit and orchid plantations, palm sugar production sites and fish farms.

Floating market

Ratchaburi (96km/59 miles), the provincial capital on the Menam Mae Khlong, was originally on the coast, but the river silted up and the sea is now some distance away. The *prang* at Wat Mahathat dates from the U Thong period, although the murals on the interior walls are from the Ayutthaya era. At **★ Phetchaburi** (126km/78 miles), Phra Nakhon Khiri, the neoclassical royal summer residence (and observatory), was built on the Wang mountain high above the town during the reign of King Mongkut. A small museum (Wednesday to Sunday, 9am–noon and 1–4pm) occupies the main hall. The religious significance of this once-important port is underlined by the town's 30 or so temples and the view of Wat Mahathat's central *prang*. Wat Yai Suwannaram, an Ayutthaya period temple further east, is also worth a visit.

THE SOUTH
0   30 km

Some 3km (2 miles) to the west of the town, a temple of meditation, Wat Khao Bandai It, sits at the foot of the hill of the same name. The hill is topped by a shrine, built by a wealthy Thai, and, situated halfway up, is the entrance to a labyrinth of caves once used by meditating monks. A Buddhist statue in the **Khao Luang cave**, 2km (1¼ miles) north of Phetchaburi, is greatly revered. It was built by Chulalongkorn in memory of his two predecessors.

The **Kaeng Krachan National Park** is the biggest in the country. A relatively unknown park with few facilities for tourism, its 1,200-m (3,930-ft) high Tenasserim range on the border with Myanmar offers excellent opportunities for observing fauna and flora. The end of the road, some 36km (22 miles) from the entrance to the park, is the starting point for several footpaths, but a guide is required.

On Cha-am beach

Cha-am (163km/101 miles from Bangkok) offers a long sandy beach. Many prosperous families own second homes or apartments in its large holiday complexes. Picnicking, walking, cycling and riding are all popular pastimes. Most of the large hotels used by European tour operators are actually in rather remote spots.

56

Hua Hin railway station and Sofitel Central

★ **Hua Hin**, 188km (116 miles) south of Bangkok, is the oldest resort on the Gulf of Thailand. At the beginning of the 20th century, the royal family discovered new hunting grounds for tigers and other big game in the jungle behind the fishing village, and a few years later they discovered the pleasures of the beach, thus ringing in the birth of Thailand's first seaside resort. Once the southern railway had been completed and the Railway Hotel (now Sofitel Central) was opened in 1923, Hua Hin started to attract the well-to-do from Bangkok. A few years later, the first golf course in the country was opened, and in 1928 Rama VII had a summer residence, Klai Kangwon ('without a care'), built in the northeast of the town. It is still used by the king and is open to visitors. The queen's palace lies some distance away, about 3km (2 miles) to the south. Sadly, the town has lost some of its earlier splendour. Apart from day trips to the offshore island of Song Toh and the rather touristy fishing village of Takeap, 6km (4 miles) to the south, there is little of interest.

Some 60km (37 miles) south of Hua Hin, the ★ **Khao Sam Roi Yot National Park** looks out over the Gulf of Thailand. Bizarrely-shaped limestone rocks, some as high as 600m (1,970ft), rise up from the green sea of rice fields. There are a number of sandy beaches and fine views over the coastline. The limestone caves make interesting destinations for excursions.

Excursion 4

Southeast to Pattaya

Pattaya seafront

The eastern coast of the Gulf of Thailand doesn't have many sandy beaches, but there are some interesting places to visit. At the heart of the region stands the resort of Pattaya, where a wide range of accommodation, restaurants and sporting and leisure activities is available. It is a good spot to spend a few days and an excellent base for trips into the hinterland and to offshore islands.

Leave Bangkok on Sukhumvit Road. Highway 3 follows the coast as far as the Cambodian border, but most buses leave from the Eastern Bus Terminal in Sukhumvit Road and travel along the multi-lane motorway (No. 34) as far as Bang Pakong in the interior. If possible, take the coast road. It may not be in very good condition, but the journey is more interesting.

Samut Prakan (26km/16 miles) lies in the Chao Phaya delta. Most of the city buses terminate here. The fortifications which originally stood guard over the river mouth were unnecessary in the 20th century and have now disappeared without trace. A single small white *chedi*, Phra Chedi Klang, on one of the islands, is all that has survived. During the 19th century, it reminded travellers arriving in the city by boat that they were entering a Buddhist country. Paying homage to a relic of Buddha continues to be the aim of an annual pilgrimage. The highlight of the pilgrims' season is the temple festival in November/December.

Most tour groups make a point of visiting the **Crocodile Farm**, 3km (2 miles) south of the town (open daily, 7am–6pm; crocodile and elephant show, Monday to Friday at 9, 10, 11am, 1, 2, 3,

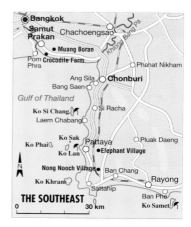

4pm, Saturday, Sunday, noon and 5pm). Over 30,000 of the creatures, which are bred solely for their leather and meat, are cooped up in concrete enclosures. On no account should visitors purchase the crocodile skin souvenirs. These contravene the CITES agreement even if the animals are reared on a commercial basis.

A visit to ★ **Muang Boran** (open daily, 8am–5pm), 6km/4 miles south of the city, is a much more rewarding experience. This extensive park contains replicas of over 80 buildings from all parts of Thailand and from all periods in the country's history. Temples, pagodas, *chedis* and palaces (one-third of their original size) have been faithfully rebuilt in appropriate surroundings. One of the main attractions is a water village with small shops. Try to allow several hours for a comprehensive tour of the site. There is also the opportunity to watch traditional dancing and other cultural events.

Ang Sila (91km/56 miles) is a small coastal village noted for its stone masons. The sound of chisels emanates from the open workshops lining the narrow road from the Sukhumvit Highway. As well as sculptures, mortars – heavy but original souvenirs – are displayed for sale outside the houses, and dried fish, another speciality, is on sale at street stalls. Between Ang Sila and Bang Saen to the southwest lie two temples: Rua Samphao, a shrine in the shape of a ship's hull, and Wat Khao Samuk, a Chinese temple noted for its comical figures.

Bang Saen (97km/60 miles) is a favourite spot for Thais from Bangkok, especially at weekends. Its long sandy beach shaded by coconut palms is an ideal place for a picnic. This traditional resort is popular with walkers, too, but avoid swimming as the quality of the water leaves much to be desired. At the Institute of Marine Science (Tuesday to Sunday, 8.30am–4pm) some familiar and unfamiliar sea creatures can be observed in the tranquillity of Thailand's biggest aquarium.

Pattaya has its peaceful moments

Part of the night-time scenery

★ **Pattaya**, the main tourist centre on the east coast, is only 136km (84 miles) from the capital. For an overview of the broad bay, take a walk to the temple on Phra Tamnak Hill at the southern end of the town. The quality of the water at Naklua in the north and Jomtien in the south has greatly improved. Only the town beach is best avoided. Facilities for watersports abound at all three beaches.

Pattaya has plenty of accommodation in all categories and is renowned for its nightlife. Hundreds of bars compete for the custom of the predominantly Western holidaymakers. The resort has acquired a reputation as a 'sun, sand and sex' resort for young people, but the authorities are now trying to transform Pattaya into a 'family resort'. The tourist infrastructure is certainly there. Many of the hotels are situated well away from the bustling town centre and can offer good facilities, including swimming pools and tropical gardens. Pattaya has a worldwide reputation for its transvestite shows; it also has a branch of the American museum chain Believe it or Not, and the Motion Master Moving Theatre offers simulated space flight. On the other hand, opera performances and symphony concerts are also staged in Pattaya.

Elephant Village lies to the east of Pattaya in a rural setting. Working elephants pose and display their skills, with Asian tourists often invited to join in the show. **Nong Nooch Village**, 17km (10 miles) to the south of Pattaya, not only has the usual elephant and cultural shows, but also a large park with attractive orchid, cacti and palm gardens. Those who wish to enjoy a relaxing walk may want to book into one of the resort's bungalows.

Accommodation in all categories

Nong Nooch dancer...

Boat excursions to the offshore coral islands are also popular. Diving, snorkelling, fishing and trips in glass-bottomed boats are the main activities available. Many visitors make for the seafood restaurants in Ko Lan, although the noise from the boats and water scooters can be distracting. For peace and quiet and unspoilt reefs, try the islands of Ko Phai and Ko Sak. Boats for a day trip to the island of Ko Samet, off Rayong, leave from the fishing village of Ban Phe.

In 1981 all the islands were declared a national park. There are many simple bungalows and restaurants by the beaches, but water supply and waste disposal can be a problem. For more comfortable accommodation, it will probably be necessary to look at the beaches on the mainland, such as the one east of Ban Phe, where you can stay in the extensive Wang Kaeo Resort (tel: 038/63 80 67, for reservations in Bangkok, tel: 02/259 41 50).

59

...and performing elephants

Art History

Opposite: guardians of Wat Pho

The damp tropical conditions combined with the effects of many wars have destroyed much of Thailand's ancient cultural heritage. Ruined temples and Buddhist statues are all that remain.

The artistic styles of central Thailand

Dvaravati (6th–10th century): The Mons established the first union of Buddhist states with cultural centres at U Thong, Nakhon Pathom and Lopburi. They fortified their towns with ditches and built temple complexes dominated by slim, bell-shaped *chedis*. Clear, symmetrical lines are the distinguishing features of the Mons' stone carvings.

Lopburi (10th–14th century): Khmer princes extended their territory westwards from Cambodia, expelled the Mons and founded the Lopburi empire. During its cultural heyday in the 12th century the rulers converted from Hinduism to Buddhism, whereupon they built the huge temple site at Angkor, now regarded as *the* architectural masterpiece of that era. Other similar, albeit smaller temples, were built on what is now Thai territory. The best known is situated in Phimai (to the northeast of Bangkok) and traces of Hindu influence are clearly visible.

61

Sukhothai (13th–15th century): During the first Thai empire, Rama Khamhaeng made Buddhism the state religion and devised the first Thai script. Although strongly influenced by the neighbouring cultures, an independent Thai culture emerged. Khmer and Dvaravati features such as the *prang* and *chedi* were incorporated into temple architecture. Highly desirable Sawankhalok pottery was fired in the kilns and some particularly harmonious Buddhas were cast in bronze in the country's workshops.

Among the ruins of Ayutthaya

Ayutthaya (14th–18th century): Splendid temples and palaces, fortresses and canals bear witness to the wealth and power of the absolutist Thai rulers. Lively trade bestowed Thai art with influences from India, China, Japan and Europe. At the beginning of the Ayutthaya period, the influences of the Khmer are apparent – severe-looking Buddha statues with angular faces. The *prangs* with their high bases, however, are slimmer and more elegant than the Khmer versions. Sukothai influences predominated at the height of the Ayutthaya era and these later formed the basis of an independent, Thai national style.

From Ayutthaya came Bangkok

Bangkok (from the 18th century): The new capital of Bangkok was built from the ruins of Ayutthaya, but the Royal Palace and temples copy closely their Ayutthaya

Royal Palace: prang and chedis

predecessors. With slimmer columns, higher gabled roofs and decorations made of new materials, such as marble slabs, porcelain and mirror fragments, the temples looked much more elegant. During the reign of Rama III, Chinese stylistic features dominated, while under Western-oriented rulers Mongkut and Chulalongkorn, European influences became apparent.

Temple architecture

Most monastery complexes or *wats* consist of a number of meeting halls around a central shrine, the *bot*. Monks are ordained in the *bot*. Eight stones, *bai semas*, mark off the border between the consecrated and unconsecrated ground. A ninth stone is located under the *bot*.

Meditating monks and tired visitors often seek refuge in the *salas* or ornate pavilions. Alongside stand stepped-roof bell-towers and the *mondhop*, where the holy scriptures are kept. A *chedi* or a *prang* tops the temple buildings. While *chedis* are bell-shaped and then crowned with a pointed spire, *prangs* taper up to a rounded tip.

Decorative details include serpents and demons

Ridges, gables and stairs are all richly decorated with dragon-headed serpents *(nagas)*, *garuda* birds, the vehicle of Indra, and the god's elephant, Erawan. Graceful half-bird, half-human *kinnara* and *kinnari* adorn the doors and walls, while fierce-looking, giant *yaksha* (demons) and even Rama's arch-enemy, Tosakan, from the *Ramayana* epic, guard the entrances.

Wall paintings

Painting developed during the Bangkok period, particularly during the reign of Rama III. Early illustrations were two-dimensional, but in the mid-19th century one or two painters started to experiment with perspective. The early life cycles of Buddha, fabled creatures from Hindu mythology and historical scenes, such as the wars against the Burmese and the arrival of Europeans in Ayutthaya, are depicted on the internal walls of the *bot*, *viharn* and along the covered walkways. Also very popular are scenes from the Ramakien *(see right)*. The finest example is to be found along the walkway at Wat Phra Kaeo.

Inlay work

This painstaking technique was first used to aggrandise temples and royal palaces during the Ayutthaya period. Later on, furniture inlaid with mother-of-pearl and other materials adorned the residences of the courtiers and wealthy businessmen. The gleaming matt inner shell of the Turban sea urchin *(cidaris)* was sliced thinly, flattened and cut to shape. It was then glued to a smoothed, wooden surface and the intervening spaces filled with thin layers of black lacquer.

The Ramakien Legend

For centuries, the peoples of southern Asia, from India to Indonesia, have been entertained by the story of the struggle between gods and demons, between good and evil, the passionate love of the beautiful Princess Sita for the hero Rama, the unshakeable loyalty of his brother and the vengeance of the gods. In the Thai version of the Indian *Ramayana* epic, the giant king Tosakan (Rawana), ruler of the island of Lanka, defeats the god Indra and then sets out to dominate the world. The gods send the immortal Vishnu to earth in human form, as the only way of putting a stop to Tosakan's ambitions.

The powerful empire of Ayutthaya was once ruled by the wise king Totsarot (Dasharatha). Vishnu is incarnated in Prince Rama, the king's oldest son. News of the heroic deeds of the young prince, his brother and loyal friend Lakshman (Lakhsmana) spread throughout the country and Rama is chosen to succeed to the throne. By applying his superhuman powers, he succeeds in winning the love of the virtuous Princess Sita. His happiness seems complete, until one of the royal concubines persuades the king to give precedence to her son and to banish Rama. Accompanied by his wife and his brother, Rama spends 14 years in a hermitage deep in a forest.

When the giant king Tosakan hears what has happened to the princess, he abducts her and takes her back to his palace in Lanka. Rama and Lakshman set off in search of Sita. They enlist the monkey king Sukrib as an ally and he places his army at Rama's disposal, under the leadership of the white monkey general Hanuman. Hanuman flies to the island and discovers Sita imprisoned in Tosakan's palace. So an army of monkeys, together with Rama and Lakshman, make for the coast close to the island. Hanuman turns himself into a bridge across the narrow straits and the battle with Tosakan's forces begins. The return of Sita seems assured as the battle with the demon king comes to a conclusion but, at the very last minute, Tosakan escapes with Sita. At this point, Hanuman cunningly wins the trust of Tosakan, uncovers the secret of the giant's strength and Rama is able to kill him at the end of a strength-sapping seven-day duel. They all finally return home to Ayutthaya in triumph and the new king abdicates in favour of his step-brother Rama.

However, after suspicions about Sita's fidelity while she was with Tosakan emerge, Rama rejects his wife and orders Lakshman to kill her. Instead, he sends her off to a hermitage in the woods where she gives birth to a baby boy. Rama soon learns of the child's existence and recognises him as his son. In the end, the rebellious giants are defeated and Rama returns to the gods.

63

Scenes from the Ramakien

Dancers at the Erawan Shrine

Performing the lakhon nai

Music and Theatre

At the classical dance and drama school in the National Theatre's Department of Fine Arts, girls begin to learn the classical *khon* mask dances and also the graceful *lakhon* style at a very young age. Only after several years of training are they able to perform the complicated steps and intricate gestures. Every movement has its own special significance, expressing a particular feeling or explaining a certain event.

In classical *khon*, the dancers wear brilliantly crafted masks and a choir performs poetic tales and songs. Almost all the stories contain elements of cruelty and symbolism, and the scenes from the *Ramayana* epic are by far the most popular.

Lakhon, in fact, covers various types of dance-drama: the popular and humorous *lakhon nok* can, like *lakhon jatri*, be seen at the Erawan or Lak Muang shrines (*see pages 16 and 46*); the harmonious and dignified *lakhon nai* was once performed only inside the palace walls and even today the dancers with their heavily made-up faces, brocade costumes and multi-layered golden crowns create an exotic atmosphere. Male roles are performed by women, who carry wings protruding from their shoulders, thus resembling garuda birds.

Dance performances are normally accompanied by a traditional *piiphaat* band whose instruments include gongs of varying sizes, two xylophones, drums, violins and wind instruments. To western ears, the music may sound strange, as the Thai octave is based on seven full-tone intervals with no semi-tones. There is no musical notation, so the musicians must learn the piece by heart.

Every Tuesday and Thursday at 8pm, the Chalerm Krung Royal Theatre (Old Siam Plaza, 66 Charoen Krung

Road, tel: 222 1352; *see page 41*) puts on shortened two-hour performances of the *Ramayana* epic with English sub-titles and a light show. Entrance 500–1,000 baht, formal dress required. At the National Theatre (Na Phratat Road, Sanam Luang; for information, tel: 224 1342 or enquire at the box office between 10am and noon), traditional *khon* and *lakhon* performances are given on the last Friday of the month from 5.30–9pm. Entrance 100–300 baht. Classical Thai dancers perform in a number of Bangkok restaurants.

It is, however, pop music that emanates from the loudspeakers of hotels and restaurants. As well as Western-style music, an original Thai-style pop has evolved. The music ranges from schmaltzy love songs to hard rock and disco. Carabou and Zuzu are two groups with a reputation for lyrics with a social conscience. *Luk grung* romantic ballads are very popular, as is *lok thung*, a type of country music influenced by Thai folklore. *Mor lam*, a singing style with guitar and mouth organ accompaniment, originated in northeast Thailand.

Muay thai – the martial arts

Thai boxing in the main Bangkok stadiums arouses great interest, mainly among men. Most Thais would not hesitate to describe this ferocious martial art as one of the prime elements of their cultural heritage. They come to not only watch, but also to gamble. The sport dates from the 16th century, when warriors were taught to use mortal blows in close combat. The king at the time, Naresuan, was famed for his bravery and is said to have defeated his Burmese counterpart using these techniques. In the following turbulent century, even the monks felt the need to learn the art of Thai boxing.

According to the rules, fists, knees, elbows and feet may all be used. Before the fight, the *ram muay* ceremony expresses deference to the fighter's guru as well as the guardian spirit of Thai boxing. Each boxer works out his own dance routine which is then performed to the accompaniment of shrill, monotonous music. As long as one of the fighters is not knocked out, the fight lasts for five rounds, each three minutes in duration with intervals of two minutes.

To watch an authentic Thai boxing match, visit either the Lumpini stadium (tel: 280 45 50; Tuesday, Friday, 6pm, Saturday 4.30pm and 8.30pm) or the Ratdamnoen stadium (tel: 281 42 05; Monday, Wednesday, 6pm, Thursday 5pm and 9pm, Sunday 2pm and 6pm). Even from the cheaper seats, there is a good view of the fight. It is also an excellent place to enjoy the atmosphere. The best fighters enter the ring at about 9pm. Fights organised in night-clubs are a poor imitation of the real thing.

65

A bout in progress

The victor

Fresh laundry for the monks

Buddhism and Spirit Worship

The stepped roofs and golden towers of temples dominate the Bangkok skyline. Shaven-headed monks in saffron robes are everywhere – in trains, in buses or simply out shopping. Early in the morning by the Marble Temple, rows of monks silently accept the donations of the faithful. The givers thank the recipients, in the hope of influencing their own *karma*, the balance between good and bad deeds that will determine their status in the next life.

Visitors to the temples are sure to find the faithful deep in prayer. The devout make offerings of lotus blossom and incense sticks and leave gifts of cash behind. Practically every adult male dons a monk's robes for at least three months of his life, thereby subjecting himself to humility and frugality and leading a disciplined and meditative lifestyle – all in the hope of improving his *karma*.

Theravada Buddhism is the faith of 95 percent of all Thais. Under its creed, every individual is responsible for his own fate. The founder of Buddhism, Prince Siddhartha Gautama, was born in 560BC in what is now Nepal. At the age of 29, he experienced human suffering and decided to live the rest of his life as an ascetic. But he found that this lifestyle could not provide the answer to his questions and so adopted a middle path. At the age of 36, during a long period of meditation under a bo tree, he discovered the 'ultimate truth'. Seven days later, Buddha, the Enlightened One, proclaimed his teaching to five disciples in Isipatana deer-park near Varanasi.

The basis of this teaching (*dharma*) is Buddha's recognition of the Four Noble Truths: the existence of suffering (*dhuka*), its cause, how to overcome it and the way to end it. The path to the suppression of suffering, the last of the Four Noble Truths, is the noble Eightfold Path. It consists of right views, right intention, right speech, right action, right livelihood, right effort, right-mindedness and right contemplation. The eighth and last stage represents an important obligation: the attainment of a state of deep concentration without succumbing to distraction.

This is the aim of the exercises in meditation in Buddhist temples. If all worldliness is left behind, the monks reach *nirvana* and can be released from the round of earthly existence and all its inherent suffering.

However deeply rooted Buddhism is in Thailand, the ancient belief in gods and spirits is still widely held. The spirit houses (*chao ti*) that are part of every Thai home provide the clearest evidence for this. They are as ornate as the residents' pocket permits. These miniature dwellings are home to the 'place lord' who reigns over a particular piece of land and has to be placated every day with gifts. *Chao ti* are sometimes seen at dangerous road junctions.

The ubiquitous spirit house

Thailand is considered full of fearful, evil spirits, and popular antidotes are amulets worn as necklaces. Spells written on cloth or on parchment can, if uttered loudly in moments of danger, help to ward off disaster.

Visiting the shrine

67

Buddhist meditation

Two types of meditation are used in Thai Buddhist monasteries: 'Samatha' and 'Vipassana'. Samatha aims to create a state of inner peace through intensive concentration. Meditation courses in Europe often teach this method, as the breathing exercises are easily learnt. Vipassana meditation has the same objective but it is achieved via 'mindfulness', a concentration on the minutiae of human perceptions.

Tourists may join meditation in some temples and may even become lay monastics. Wat Mahathat near Sanam Luang (Section Five, tel: 02-222 60 11), offers daily meditation from 7–10am, 1–4pm and 6–8pm, plus a course in English from 4–6pm every second Saturday. On the first Sunday of the month, at 2–6pm, the World Fellowship of Buddhists (616 Benjasiri Park, Soi Medhinivet, Sukhum-vit Road Soi 24, tel: 02-661 128 489) offers courses in English, while House of Dhamma (26/9 Lat Phrao Soi 15, tel: 02-511 04 39) offers classes from 2–5pm on the second, third and fourth Sundays.

Outside Bangkok try the Wat Vivekasrom Vipassana Centre (Ban Suan, Chonburi, tel: 038-283 766), Bunkanjajaram Meditation Centre (Jomtien Beach, Pattaya, tel: 038-231 865), Wat Asokaram (Samut Prakan, tel: 02-395 0003), Wongsanit Ashram (Nakhon Nayok, tel: 02-546 1518) or Suan Mokkh (Surat Thani, fax: 077-431 597). The Spirit in Education Movement has 10-day 'Deep Ecology' forest walks in Kanchanaburi, Chiang Mai and Chiang Rai (fax: 02-580 3711).

Buddhas in Wat Mahathat

Festivals and Folklore

Main festivals

End of February/beginning of March: Magha Puja is celebrated on the full moon in the third lunar month to commemorate Buddha's preaching to 1,250 enlightened monks. The faithful make the prayer of the 'threefold jewel' and then walk round the *bot* three times.

February to April: Dragon fights. Like everywhere else in the country, colourful paper kites adorn the sky at this time of year. Competitions are held on the Sanam Luang and in Lumpini Park. Great skill is required to control the dragons. The task for *chu-la*, the great male dragon, is to wrestle *pakpao*, the nimble female with the long tail, down to the ground.

6 April: Chakri Day. A public holiday commemorating the founding of the ruling dynasty. Celebrations at the Wat Phra Keo.

13/14 April: The Songkran Festival marks the beginning of the new lunar year. In the monasteries, Buddha images are sprinkled with water and, as the fun escalates, family, friends and passers-by also often get a soaking. The more water is splashed around, the more rain will fall in the coming year. No-one escapes, so leave valuable cameras in the hotel. Songkran means change. Birds and fish are released, sworn enemies are reconciled and new resolutions made. Many Thais return to their home province to celebrate Songkran and Bangkok can be quieter than normal.

5 May: Coronation Day is a private royal affair but also a public holiday.

Mid-May: Visakha Puja, an important Buddhist festival lasting three days at the time of the full moon in the sixth lunar month. It commemorates the birth, enlightenment and death of Buddha. Candle processions take place around the temple *bots*.

May: The Ploughing Ceremony marks the official start of the rice-planting season and this event in the Sanam Luang is always presided over by the king. Monks hand the farmers rice seeds which are then scattered over the fields.

July: At the full moon, Asanha Puja, the day that Buddha first preached to his disciples, is celebrated in every temple in the country. The period of fasting (Khao Parnsa) begins on the next day and ends three months later in October with the Ork Parnsa festival. The fasting period, coinciding with the rainy season (*parnsa* = 'rain'), is when young men around the age of 20 retire to a monastery for three months and are ordained as lay monks.

12 August: The queen's birthday is marked by a number of religious ceremonies. In the morning the queen gives offerings to the monks.

Loy Kraythong

7–16 October: Chinese Vegetarian Festival. Nightly, in temples along Sampeng Lane, there are Chinese opera, carnival rides and heaps of vegetarian food and delicious sweets found at no other time of year.

23 October: This day marks the death of Chulalongkorn, the fifth king of the Chakri dynasty. Students lay wreaths before his statue in front of the parliament building.

End October/beginning November: Loy Krathong is celebrated on the night of the full moon. It is one of the country's most enchanting festivals, a night when small candle- and incense-laden boats made from the trunks of banana trees (*krathongs*) are launched into the rivers and canals to ask for blessings. In Bangkok, the people throng to the banks of the Chao Phaya; by the khlongs of Thonburi, the celebrations are more modest affairs.

5 December: The king's birthday is commemorated with parades along Ratdamnoen Avenue and celebrations at the Wat Phra Kaeo.

10 December: Constitution Day is a public holiday.

Temple festivals

A large temple festival takes place in every *wat*. It can last several days and attract many devout Buddhists. Prayers and processions accompany the celebrations and a fair is often held within the temple grounds. In the evenings, the visitors are entertained with drama and music. The main temple festivals in the Bangkok area are as follows:

February: Phra Buddhist Festival in the Wat Buddhabaht in Saraburi, 130km (80 miles) north of the capital.

End October/beginning November: Phra Chedi Klang Nam Festival in Samut Prakan, about 20km (12 miles) south of Bangkok.

November: Golden Mountain Festival in the Wat Saket in the city centre.

November: Phra Pathom Chedi Festival in Nakhon Pathom, 60km (37 miles) west of Bangkok.

Festival colours

Food and Drink

Thai cuisine is now widely recognised as one of the finest in the world and, although it is often pungent and spicy, there really is a great deal more to it than hot spices. Burnt tongues are relieved more successfully with rice (*khao*) than water. This staple food is a principal component of every main meal, with white rice (*khao plao*) usually served as a side dish, while rice soup (*khao tom*) is traditionally eaten at breakfast. *Khao phat* (fried rice) is an economical main course. The other ingredients in a dish are listed after the rice: *gai* is chicken, *pla* fish, *pu* crayfish/lobster, *gung* crab. So to order fried rice with chicken, simply say *khao phat gai*.

Do try *tom yam*- or *tom kha*-soups flavoured with kaffir lime leaves, lemon grass and fresh coriander leaves. Ginger and coconut milk are added to *kha*-soups. A fish sauce (*nam pla*) is usually used in place of salt in Thai cooking. The basis for the different types of hot curries (yellow, red and green) is a mix of chilis, crab paste, garlic, lemon grass and other spices, which are crushed in a mortar and then cooked with meat and vegetables in coconut milk.

Spicy chicken soup

71

Given the extreme heat during the day, the local people keep going with snacks such as noodle soup, fried rice, baked bananas or sweet cakes – all freshly prepared. The main meal, comprising meat or fish with vegetables, is served in the evening. The cook will probably try to combine a mild dish, such as a soup, with a hot curry or a pan-fried dish.

Those who normally shun hot food should stick with Chinese dishes. In the street restaurants, they serve *salapau*, a light, steamed bread roll filled with, among other things, sweet strips of pork. *Kanom djieb* are, like Chinese *wan ton*, filled with a mixture of chopped prawns and meat and then dipped in a spicy sauce. *Khao man gai* (chicken rice) is another very popular dish. Together with a delicious chicken broth, the meat is served on rice which has been cooked in stock. The meat is dipped in sauce before being eaten. *Ped dang*, fried duck on rice, is served in a similar way, but garnished with cucumber slices and pickled ginger.

Thai food is eaten with a spoon in the right hand and a fork in the left. Porcelain spoons are served with noodle soups and chopsticks with Chinese dishes.

There is a wide choice of fruit and much of what is offered may be unfamiliar. As well as bananas, pineapples and mandarin oranges, there are ripe green mangoes, apple-sized violet-coloured mangosteen and small, bright longan, sold in bunches like the red rambutan. The durian fruit with its pungent smell is unmistakable.

Fast food on the streets

Where bananas taste of bananas

Drinks

Thai whisky (mainly Mekong) is the most popular alcoholic drink. It is served with soda or cola. Beer is brewed in Thailand. Soft drinks, fruit juices and the juice of the young coconut, as well as mineral water, tea and coffee, are available everywhere.

Bangkok is a culinary paradise with something to offer every taste and every pocket. A leaflet entitled 'Bangkok – Dining and Entertainment' is often found in hotels and shopping centres. If dishes are priced according to weight (mainly fish), then the price should be agreed beforehand, especially if your *tuk-tuk* or taxi driver recommended the restaurant.

Courses in Thai cooking

It does not take long to become addicted to Thai food but by then it will probably be time to go home. Using a wok is not difficult and there are plenty of good books about Thai cooking on sale. However, to be taught by an expert is the best way to conjure up the authentic Thai taste and a number of courses in Thai cooking skills are available, if time and money permit.

There are courses lasting one to five days on offer at the Oriental Hotel (tel: 02-236 04 00, fax: 02-459 75 87). Thai House (Nonthaburi, 22km/14 miles) west of the city centre, tel: 02-280 07 40, fax: 02-280 07 41) also teaches Thai cooking, and accommodates participants in a traditional teak house during the four-day course. Winda offers Thai and Indian cooking lessons at Mrs Balbir's, 155/18 Sukhumvit Soi 11 (tel: 02-651 04 98, fax: 02-255 42 35).

Fast food Thai-style

A sea of seafood
Satay: the Malaysian influence

As most women go out to work, many Thais eat at snack bars on their way to and from home. The dishes are superb, as all the stall-holders try to keep their regular customers satisfied. Dozens of small stalls in the 'food centres' or 'food courts' (as they are called locally) offer a wide range of reasonably priced dishes. These are all prepared in front of the customer, who can eat the crispy spring rolls, hot curries or delicious soups at little tables.

Most of Bangkok's food markets were in the open air, but are now in shopping centres. The best food court, which offers a superb culinary tour of Thailand, is in the Emporium Department Store on Sukhumvit Road. Food courts gained custom from office workers and middle-class shoppers (who might formerly have eaten at restaurants) following the Asian financial meltdown in 1997. They are now sometimes known as 'IMF food courts' – and appealing meals can be had for about US$1.

The following restaurant suggestions are listed according to three categories: $$$ = expensive; $$ = moderate; $ = inexpensive.

Culinary collage

Thai restaurants

$$$**Bussaracum**, 139 Pan Road, between Silom Road and Sathon Nua Road, tel: (02) 266 6312-8. Authentic Thai cuisine, offering a feast for the eyes and a treat for the taste buds. Benjarong branch in the Dusit Thani Hotel. $$$**Sala Rim Naam**, Oriental Hotel, tel: (02) 236 04 00. A boat takes guests across the river for excellent food and the Thai dancing. $$$**White Elephant**, in the JW Marriott, Sukhumvit Soi 2, tel: (02) 656 7700. $$**Cabbages & Condoms**, Sukhumvit Road Soi 12, tel: (02) 229 46 10 (daily 11am–10pm). Excellent Thai cuisine in a delightful garden or the well-cooled interior. $$**Somboon Pochana**, 169/7–11 Surawong Road, tel: (02) 233 31 04. Seafood specialities: perhaps the best, and messiest, is *puu phad phong karee* (sea-crab fried in curry sauce). $**Ngwanlee Langsuan**, 101/25–26 Soi Langsuan at Sarasin Road across from Lumpini Park, tel: (02) 250 09 36. Popular Chinese and Thai seafood in a modest setting.

Free giveaways at Cabbages and Condoms

Stuffed mussels

Other Asian restaurants

$$**LeDalat Indochine**, 14 Sukhumvit Soi 23, tel: (02) 661 7967-8. Vietnamese specialties. $$**Kobe Steak House**, 460 Siam Square Soi 7, Rama I Road, tel: (02) 251 13 36. $$**RiceMill**, Marriott Royal Garden Riverside, tel: (02) 476 0021-2. Enjoy the cruise-like free boat trip from River City. Chinese. $$**Himali Cha Cha Restaurant**, 1229/11 New Road, tel: (02) 235 15 69, near the Oriental Hotel. Classic North Indian cuisine, plus vegetarian and Muslim dishes. $$**Koreana**, Siam Square Soi 7, tel: (02) 252 93 98, and Sukhumvit Soi 11, tel: (02) 253 8894. The oldest and biggest Korean restaurants in town.

Fish with vegetables

Dinner cruises

$$$Dinner Cruise, tel: (02) 234 55 99 (daily at 6pm) and River Sightseeing, tel: (02) 437 40 47 (daily at 7.30pm) from River City. Guests from all over the world enjoy a multi-course traditional Thai menu while the boat slowly cruises through the Bangkok night.

$$Kanab Nam, tel: (02) 433 66 11. This restaurant serving original Thai cuisine is very popular with the locals. Restaurant boats leave at 7pm and 8pm from the Thonburi side of the Krung Thong Bridge. *A la carte* meals should be ordered in the restaurant before departure. Small surcharge payable for the boat trip.

$Yok Yor, tel: (02) 282 18 29. Boats leave from the Wisut Kasat pier at 8pm. Authentic Thai food served. Has a reputation for very hot dishes.

Restaurants outside Bangkok

Ayutthaya

$$Ruenpae, 36/1 U Thong Road. Freshwater fish are the speciality of this floating restaurant. Very popular with tour groups.

$Racha, 5/4 Rojana Road. Garden restaurant serving Thai cuisine. Live music in the evenings.

Another way to serve prawns

Khao Yai National Park

$$Khao Yai Garden Lodge, Kilometer 7, 135 Thanon Thanarat, Pak Chong, tel: (044) 313 567. German-built complex with clean rooms. Set in large gardens with a simple restaurant. The owner also organises tours.

Kanchanaburi

$Evening food market by the banks of the river. Floating restaurants on the river, in the town and by the bridge.

Hua Hin

Some restaurants by the beach, to the south of the pier, serve fresh seafood. Try the **Charoen Pochana**. The night market in Dechanuchit Road is another alternative. This is a good place to sample the full range of Thai food and to look for souvenirs.

Sweet delights

Pattaya

$$Ruen Thai, 485/3 Moo 10, Pattaya Second Road. Superb Thai dishes served in a large and beautiful garden. Classical dance performances on some evenings.

$$Bavaria House, South Pattaya and Bavaria II in a beer tent, Central Arcade/Pattaya Second Road. German cooking and draught beer to the accompaniment of brass band music.

$$Akamon, 468/19 Pattaya Second Road, North Pattaya. Japanese food at reasonable prices.

Shopping

No one could possibly leave Thailand without buying a souvenir of some description. With so much to choose from in the shops, markets and street stalls, even the most miserly tourist is likely to find something irresistible.

World-famous **Thai silk** is produced in varying qualities. It does not have a smooth surface and it is a little heavier than the Chinese variety. The bulk of the silk comes from factories but, during the dry season in the northeast and north, women make the traditionally patterned material on hand looms. One labour-intensive technique known as *mudmee* produces a beautiful, but expensive fabric. The threads are coloured using natural dyes before being woven into special patterns.

The name of Jim Thompson is inextricably linked with Thai silk (*see page 46*). His name can be seen on many shops, especially in Suriwong Road and in the Isetan Department Store. Silk shops can also be found in the Siam Centre along Rama I Road. Many other fabrics are sold at the weekend markets and tailors are happy to produce made-to-measure suits within 24 hours.

There are restrictions on the export of **antiques** (*see page 90*), but wooden fakes modelled on antique sculptures make lovely home decor items. Wooden furniture includes cabinets, tables, dining room and bedroom sets or something as simple as a tray. The carving tends to be heavy and the pieces are generally large.

Bangkok's **jewellery** trade has a worldwide reputation and its headquarters are housed in the glass-walled 55-storey Bangkok Gem and Jewellery Tower in Suriwong Road. It contains a fully-computerised international jewellery and diamond exchange and members of the public are welcome to visit the jewellers. The gem-cutting factories are also happy for tourists to visit and make

Woodcarving tends to be heavy

75

Silk comes in many colours

Fans make popular souvenirs

Cultural contrasts

purchases. Most gems are imported, but a few are mined locally at Bo Phloi near Kanchanaburi, Bo Rai near the Cambodian border and Chantaburi on the east coast, where modern methods are used to unearth rubies and sapphires.

The choice of souvenirs in Bangkok's shops and markets is endless. Brightly-coloured T-shirts and other cotton goods are among the best bargains, but other popular items include lacquered vases and boxes (*thai krueng khoen*) made from wood or bamboo cane and finished in black and gold, matt green Celadon pottery, bronze cutlery and brass temple bells, bright umbrellas and fans, dolls and masks, pictures, leatherware and cassettes with traditional and international music. Pirated brand names are another feature of Bangkok's markets.

In the Royal Folk Arts and Crafts Centre near Bang Sai (*see page 49*), under the patronage of the queen, artisans are trained in the **traditional crafts**. Their best creations are sold in the Chitralada shops, which have branches in the Oriental Hotel, Hilton Hotel, the airport, the Royal Palace and Vimarnmek Palace.

Bangkok is bookworm heaven for those seeking books on anywhere in Asia. The major **bookshop chains** in Bangkok are: Books Kinokuniya, Emporium Shopping Complex, 622 Sukhumvit Road (the best bookshop in town); Asia Books, 221 Sukhumvit Road, branches in the Peninsula Plaza (Ratdamri Road), the Landmark (Sukhumvit Road near Soi 4) and World Trade Centre; Bookazine, CP Tower, 313 Silom Road, branches in Siam Square and Pattaya (for foreign newspapers); White Lotus, 11/2 Sukhumvit Soi 58 (tel: 02-311 21 77): collectors' books on Thailand and Asia.

Shopping centres

There are simply dozens of attractive, modern shopping centres. The biggest is the World Trade Centre with the Zen Department Store (Rama I Road/Ploenchit Road). Genuine designer boutiques are concentrated mainly in the Peninsula Plaza (Ratdamri Road), while River City near the riverside Royal Orchid Hotel specialises in antiques, handicrafts and silk. The Central Department Store (Ploenchit Road) is the city's oldest department store and it has a smaller branch in the Silom Complex near the Dusit Thani Hotel.

Bangkok's markets

The markets of southeast Asia have a special appeal. Lively, chaotic and loud, with exotic smells and fascinating insights, they are a strong draw. Overflowing market stalls display the full range of tropical food and there is nowhere better to observe at close quarters the daily lives of the local people.

Traditional markets can still be found in the heart of the modern capital, but many old markets are disappearing and being replaced by tower blocks, air-conditioned shopping centres and Western-style supermarkets, where the fruit and vegetables are laid out in well-lit, chilled display stands fitted with sprinkler systems.

Even the textile market in Banglampoo has been affected by the competition from the smart city-centre shops, and attempts are being made to exclude all markets from the central Rattanakosin area. Even the biggest market, the Chatuchai Weekend Market, in the north of the city, is to be replaced by a three-storey market building. Hopefully, there will be attempts to retain or revitalise some of the traditional markets. Old market halls, such as the Old Siam Plaza in Pahurat, have been carefully restored. The most important of the remaining markets is **Banglampoo** (Khaosan Road and surrounding area): fabrics, household goods, food stalls and souvenir market.

Pak Khlong Talaad for fruit…

Bangrak (at the end of Silom Road, near the Shangri-La Hotel): material, fruit and vegetables.

Lang Krasdang (by the Khlong Lord around the Royal Hotel): night market every day except Thursday. Second-hand goods, handicrafts, electrical goods, jewellery and knick-knacks.

Pahurat (Indian quarter): large, covered clothes and textile market. Everything for the tailor. Mainly Sikh traders.

Pak Khlong Talaad (by the Menam Chao Phaya west of the Memorial Bridge): large market selling vegetables, fruit and flowers. Open all day.

…and flowers

Patpong (Patpong Road and side streets): night market from 4pm. Large range of souvenirs, handicrafts and pirated goods.

Pratunam – or what remains of it (Ratprarop/Petchburi Road): covered market, fabrics, household goods. Many Indian traders.

Sampeng Lane (Soi Wanit, Chinatown): narrow street with many Chinese shops. Mainly fabrics, food, jewellery and temple offerings.

Thewet (where the Khlong Krung Kasem opens into the Menam Chao Phaya): flowers south of the canal, fruit and vegetables to the north. Household goods etc in a market hall further east.

Thieves' Market (between Charoen Krung, Yaowarat, Chakrawat Road and the canal): brassware, machine parts, musical instruments and furniture.

Weekend market (Chatuchak Park, north of the town): Bangkok's biggest market (Saturday and Sunday) attracts 20,000 visitors to 8,000 fully-stocked stalls. See, smell and taste every imaginable kind of fruit, food and drink. New and old, mass-produced goods and hand-made crafts.

Crafts at the Weekend Market

Nightlife

Pulsating Patpong

A stroll along the 250-m (275-yd) long Patpong Road and down the nearby side streets is just as much a part of a trip to Bangkok as a trip round the red light-district would be part of a visit to Amsterdam. Who could possibly return home without having seen for themselves the dimly-lit clubs with their go-go dancers, the massage parlours and the transvestite bars – the dens of iniquity for which the city is so famous? The go-go bars on the ground floor are usually harmless enough, but many a tourist has regretted going to one of the shows upstairs. The government has sought to outlaw child prostitution (anyone under the age of 18) and clients of under-age sex workers are now subject to fines and jail sentences.

A bustling night market

There is always plenty going on in the night markets, although many of the stalls sell counterfeit designer clothes and overpriced handicrafts.

Many restaurants also provide entertainment, often in the form of traditional dance performances, and several companies offer dinner cruises on the Chao Phaya (*see page 74*). Alternatives to the bars in Patpong Road are the night-clubs in the big hotels, discotheques, karaoke bars and pubs with live music, all of which begin to fill up a little later than the restaurants. They are concentrated in Soi Lang Suan and Soi Sarasin, north of Lumpini Park. And when you emerge in the early hours, why not try a delicious noodle soup, freshly prepared at a street-corner food stand?

The monthly magazine *Metro* keeps residents and visitors informed about what is new in the restaurant, pub and night-club scene.

Hotel bars with live music

Bamboo Bar in the Oriental Hotel, 48 Oriental Avenue. The **Lobby Bar** in the Shangri-La Hotel, 89 Soi Wat Suanplu. **Tiara Cocktail Bar** in the Dusit Thani, 946 Rama IV Road. **The Bar** in the Regent Hotel, 155 Ratdamri Road.

Pubs with live music

Hard Rock Café, 424/3–6 Siam Square Soi 11, Rama I Road, tel: (02) 251 07 92. Branch of the worldwide chain. Live music from 9.30pm. **Round Midnight**, 106/12 Soi Lang Suan, north of Lumpini Park, tel: (02) 251 06 52. Live music in the evening, Tuesday to Sunday. **Spasso**, Grand Hyatt Erawan, 494 Ratdamri Road. Live music, practically every day. **Old West**, 231/17 Soi Sarasin, tel: (02) 252 95 10. Live music every evening. **Brown Sugar**, 231/19–20 Soi Sarasin, tel: (02) 250 0103. Live jazz every evening. **Saxophone**, 3/8 Phya Tai Road. Jazz standards near the Victory Monument.

Discotheques, videotheques and cabaret

Taurus, Sukhumvit Soi 26, 6.30pm–2am. Hot, trendy, multi-level disco and videotheque. **Narcissus**, 112 Sukhumvit Soi 23, 9pm–2am. Ostentatious, art deco. **Legends**, Dusit Thani, 946 Rama 4 Road. Dance with the Thai elite. **Lucifers**, Patpong Soi 1, midnight–4am. A grotto-like escape from the Patpong go-go scene, for serious techno-heads. **Radio City**, Patpong Soi 1, 5pm–2am. Home of Elvis and Tom Jones impersonators. **Rome Club**, Patpong 3. Chic, gay videotheque, drag show, 9pm–2am. **Calypso**, Asia Hotel, Phya Thai Road. 'Boys Will Be Girls', Thailand's Spice Girls, 8.15 and 9.45pm. **Studio Music Style**, Sukhumvit Soi 24, from noon on weekends. Discos, karaoke rooms and pubs under one roof.

Party time

Outside Bangkok

Ayutthaya

Knock on Wood, opposite the Ayutthaya Grand Hotel. Locals and holidaymakers meet here for live music and draught beer.

Kanchanaburi

Apache Saloon, Saengchuto Road, with Country & Western music and live music Thai-style. Floating discos, mainly at the weekend.

Pattaya

Pattaya is famous for its transvestite shows. Popular venues include the **Alcazar** (Pattaya 2 Road, tel: 038-428 746) and **Tiffany** (Pattaya Sport Bazaar Building, tel: 038-429 642). The town's biggest disco, **Palladium**, can accommodate 6,000 guests.

Pattaya for transvestite shows
Apache Saloon, Kanchanaburi

Getting There

By plane

Bangkok is served by more than 40 international airlines, including its national carrier Thai Airways, which lands at the city's Don Muang airport. Direct flights from Europe take approximately 12 hours, while from the United States (West Coast) the journey is about 18 hours. Bangkok is also well connected with many cities in Asia, the Middle East and Oceania. Remember to reconfirm your return flight at least 72 hours before departure.

Bangkok International Airport (Don Muang) lies 22km (14 miles) north of the city. A free minibus shuttle service runs between the international and domestic terminals, but a covered walkway also links the two. A banking service, a hotel booking facility, a post office and a tourist information service are all available at the airport.

The journey by car from Don Muang airport to the city centre takes 1–2 hours depending on how bad the traffic jams are. For this reason, many business travellers choose to arrive in Bangkok late at night when traffic is light. Go to the official taxi booking counters at the arrival hall where there is a choice of a private limousine, an airport taxi or public taxi for the drive to the city. You will be issued a coupon upon payment. Be prepared to pay a small surcharge to the driver to use the expressway that takes you to Bangkok. Airport buses at a fixed fare of 70 baht (US$2) have established routes – A1 to Pratunam, Ratdamri, Silom, A2 to Phahol Yothin, Ratdamnoen, Sanam Luang, Khaosan, Banglampoo, and A3 to Suk-humvit, Thonglor – and stop at both international terminals and the adjacent domestic terminal. Trains to Hualampong, Bangkok's central rail terminal, leave from Don Muang railway station opposite the airport, but bus or taxi is a better choice for most travellers.

Traffic can be a nightmare   **81**

By rail

There is a daily train link between Singapore and Bangkok via Kuala Lumpur and Butterworth in Malaysia. The same route is covered by the Eastern & Oriental Express, which offers a nostalgic travel experience at appropriately high prices. For more information, call Bangkok, tel: (662) 216 8661-2; UK, tel: (020) 7805 5100; US, tel: (800) 524 2420; or Singapore, tel: (065) 392 3500.

By road

It is possible to travel by road from Malaysia, either by taxi or tour buses which serve Singapore and Malaysia with Hat Yai in south Thailand. The opening of the Friendship Bridge linking Laos and Nong Khai in 1994 has made road crossings between Laos and Thailand possible.

The old and the new

Getting Around

By bus, taxi and tuk-tuk

Non-air-conditioned city buses operate on fixed routes at a 3.50 baht fixed fare. Otherwise fares are set according to distance, beginning at 6 and 8 baht (older blue and newer orange air-con buses). Guaranteed seating Mercedes micro-buses charge 20 baht. Destinations are in Thai, so foreigners must rely on bus numbers. Buy a city plan and route map at travel agents, bookshops or hotels.

Most taxis in Bangkok are fitted with taximeters. Look for the large sign 'TaxiMeter' on the roof of the vehicle. If travelling in a taxi without a taximeter, agree the fare with the driver before setting off. Many 'TaxiMeter' drivers try to negotiate an all-in price, but passengers are under no obligation to make such an agreement, and they should make it clear that they will abide by the metered price. Usually the clock will be promptly switched on. If not, there are always plenty of other taxis. Few drivers speak English, so it is essential to write the destination in Thai, but always ensure that the driver really understands what is meant and knows where it is. Passengers who get the impression that the driver does not know where to go should look for another taxi – many taxi drivers do not know Bangkok any better than their foreign fares. After dark, many drivers insist on locking all the doors. Taxis are a cheap way of getting around: the basic fare is only 35 baht.

It is impossible to imagine Bangkok without its *tuk-tuks*, noisy, motorised three-wheelers with covered seats. In view of the poor air quality in Bangkok city centre, they are really only suitable for short journeys. Prices must be agreed beforehand, as *tuk-tuk* drivers are prone to charging tourists extortionate prices; they may also try to lure their fares into shops where they can earn a small commission.

By boat

Express boats and ferries moor alongside many of the riverside piers (*ta*). While the ferries with standing room only are just for crossing the river, the express boats cover the stretch between Nonthaburi in the north and the Krung Thep bridge in the south (every 10 to 30 minutes from 6am to 7pm). These large boats with plenty of seating below deck are a quick and economical way of getting from Sanam Luang to Chinatown.

Khlong boats (*rua hang yao*) ply up and down the *khlongs* between Bangkok and Thonburi. They stop when requested at both private and public

82

EXPRESS BOATS

0   1000 m

● Pier (Ta)

Raj Withee Rd.

Chao Phaya

Wasukri

Thewet

Sri Ayutthaya Rd.

Wisut Kasat

Samsen

Krung

Menam

Wat Sam Phaya

Phra Pin Klao

Banglamphoo

Ratdamnoen Nok Rd.

Kasem Rd.

Thonburi Station

Phra Athit

Thonburi Station

Phra Nok

Ratdamnoen

Rachini

Klang Rd.

Khlong Mahanak

Maharat

Chang

Bamrung

Muang Road

Wat Phra Kaeo

Chak

Royal Palace

Charoen

Rd.

Krung

Thien

Kasem

Yaowarat

Road

Rachini

Saphan Phut

Rajawongse Road

Maha

Prachathipok Rd.

Memorial Br.

Tsaraphap Road

Khl. Bangkok

Harbour Department

Lard Ya Road

Si Phaya

Wat Muang Kae

Wongwian Yai Station

Krung Thonburi Road

Oriental

Taksin Bridge

Sathorn

places. Prices vary from 5 and 20 baht according to route, time of day and distance. They operate from Chang pier along the Khlong Bangkok Noi and Khlong Bangkok Yai as far as Bang Kruay and Bang Yai, from Thien pier along the Khlong Mon and from Saphan Phut pier along the Khlong Bang Waek. In Bangkok, they use the sewage channels from Phanfa pier by the Golden Mount along the Khlong Saen Saeb into the eastern suburbs and from the Phra Sumen Fort along the Khlong Banglampoo, Khlong Mahanak and Khlong Krung Kasem to the main station. These boats can also be hired for private tours from the Chang, Thien and Oriental piers and other landing stages.

By elevated train

Bangkok's traffic congestion is improving somewhat, owing to improved management and mass transit. In late 1999, the 24-km (15-mile) Bangkok Mass Transit Company's elevated trains network began serving downtown Bangkok with two intersecting lines, from Mo Chit (Phahol Yothin Road near the Northern Bus Terminal) to Sukhumvit Soi Onnut in the southeast, and from Saladaeng-Silom to Sathorn Road (Taksin Bridge) in the southwest. Stations include Victory Monument, Siam Square, National Stadium, Chitlom, Nana and Ekamai (Eastern Bus Terminal). Construction has also begun on an underground to open in stages beginning in 2002.

Relaxation and chaos

Getting out of Bangkok

Buses leave for all parts of the country from the city's bus stations. The Eastern Bus Terminal, opposite Sukhumvit Soi 63 (Ekamai), tel (02) 391 25 04, serves the east coast, eg Pattaya, Rayong, Samet. For Ayutthaya, Chiang Mai, Nakorn Ratchasima and elsewhere in central, northern and northeast Thailand, go to Mo Chit 2 terminal (also Mo Chit *mai* or 'new' in Thai) near Chatuchak in Kampaengpaet Road, tel: (02) 936 29 96, 936 2841-8. The south and west, including Damnoen Saduak, Kanchanaburi, Hua Hin and Phuket, are served by the Southern Bus Terminal, Phra Pin Klao Road, tel: (02) 435 12 00.

The red, non-air-conditioned standard buses are economical and stop everywhere, but the seating is cramped. The blue, air-conditioned buses are more comfortable and passengers can enjoy videos, light meals and snacks. The new VIP buses with plush seats, plenty of leg room and toilets offer even greater comfort.

Ayutthaya

Plenty of buses leave from the Northern Bus Terminal in Bangkok for the bus station, 4km (2½ miles) from Ayutthaya. Minibuses from the Victory Monument in Bangkok stop by Ayutthaya's central market.

Bus services are good

Kanchanaburi
Buses leave regularly from Bangkok's Southern Bus Terminal. Plenty of buses depart for the main tourist destinations from Kanchanaburi's bus station near the market.

Hua Hin
Buses leave every 20 minutes from the Southern Bus Terminal in Bangkok. Four-hour journey.

Pattaya
Regular bus service from the Eastern and Mo Chit 2 bus terminals in Bangkok, as well as from the airport and some hotels in Bangkok. Three-hour journey to Pattaya.

Getting out by rail
Bangkok is at the hub of Thailand's railway network. The main station for long-distance trains is **Hua Lamphong**. A few railcars leave from Thonburi station for Kanchanaburi. Trains are slower and more expensive than the overland buses, but they are more comfortable. However, they tend to be very popular so it is advisable to make a reservation in good time. The Advance Booking Office in Bangkok is situated at the main station, tel: (02) 224 77 88, 220 43 34, fax: (02) 225 60 68. Open daily, 8am–4pm.

Most long-distance trains have second-class sleeping compartments with comfortable beds and also a dining car, so overnight travel presents no particular problems. Fares vary according to the type of train, from local stopping trains, inter-city trains with second- and third-class compartments, up to express trains with air-conditioned first- and second-class seating and expensive, modern express diesel railcars (sprinters) with comfortable reclining seats. The Eastern and Oriental Express, a luxury train in the old style, runs from Bangkok to Singapore two to five times a month, and from Bangkok to Chiang Mai one to three times a month. Expensive, but truly unforgettable. Tel: (02) 216 8661-2, fax: (02) 216 86 63.

Ayutthaya
Trains leave about every hour from Bangkok main station, stopping at the centrally located station by the river.

Kanchanaburi
Two trains a day from Thonburi station in Bangkok. Special trains at the weekend to Nam Tok via Kanchanaburi.

Hua Hin
All trains that head south from Bangkok stop at the station in the town centre. Apart from the express trains, they also stop at Nakhon Pathom, Ratchaburi and Phetchaburi.

Hua Hin station

Facts for the Visitor

Visas

Visitors from most countries are issued with 2- or 4-week entry permits on arrival and upon presentation of a passport and a ticket for the return or onward journey. Entry permits cannot be extended while you are in Thailand. It is advisable to check with a Thai embassy or consulate in your country before departure.

If you are planning a longer stay, apply for either a 60-day tourist visa or 30-day transit visa from your Thai embassy or consulate overseas. These can be extended at the Immigration Office in Bangkok (tel: 287 3101/0) for a nominal fee.

Customs

There is ban on all firearms, pornographic materials and narcotics. Duty-free allowances for each visitor are one litre of wine or spirits and up to 200 cigarettes (or 250gm of cigars). Certain species of plants, vegetables and fruits are prohibited.

The export of antiques and Buddha statues of any age is forbidden. In the markets of Bangkok, rare species and products made from rare species such as turtles, crocodiles, giant monitor lizards, pythons and elephants are sold, but under the CITES agreement, the export of such items is strictly forbidden. They may not be imported into Europe and, if found at customs, such souvenirs will be confiscated and punitive fines imposed.

Tourist information

Visitors should contact the Tourism Authority of Thailand. **In the UK**: TAT, 49 Albemarle Street, London WIX 3FE, tel: (020) 7499 7679 (information line, tel: 0839 300 800), fax: (020) 7629 5519.

Don't miss the boat!

In the US: TAT, 611 North Larchmont Boulevard, 1st Floor, Los Angeles, CA 90010, tel: (323) 461 9814, fax: (323) 461 9834, e-mail: tatla@ix.netcom.com; 1 World Trade Center, Suite 3729, New York, NY 10048, tel: (212) 432 0433-5, fax: (212) 912 0920.

In Thailand: The main Tourism Authority of Thailand (TAT) office is at Le Concorde Building, 202 Ratchadaphisek Road, tel: (02) 694 1222, fax: (02) 694 1220-1, website: www.tat.or.th, e-mail: center@tat.or.th. TAT's Tourist Assistance Centre, tel: 1155, answers questions and doubles as the main contact in case of a police emergency. Some provincial TAT offices are:

Ayutthaya: Si Sanphet Road, near the Chao Sam Phya National Museum, tel: (035) 246 076-7, fax: 246078.

Kanchanaburi: Saengchuto Road, tel/fax: (034) 511 200.

Hua Hin: 114 Phetchkasem Road, tel: (032) 511 402.

Pattaya: 809 Moo 10 Phatamnak Road, tel: (038) 427 667, fax: 429 113.

No limit on foreign currency

86

Currency and exchange

There are no restrictions on the import of foreign currency, whether in the form of cash or cheques. However, cash amounts above US$ 10,000 must be declared on entry. Up to 50,000 baht may be exported; other currencies may be exported in unrestricted amounts.

The national currency is the baht, which is divided into 100 satangs. The currency is denominated into 1,000 (gray), 500 (purple), 100 (red), 50 (blue), 20 (green) and 10 (brown) baht notes. Coins include 25 and 50 satangs, and 1, 5 and 10 bahts. Following the currency devaluation in mid-1997 the exchange rate stabilised in 1998–9 to approximately 36–38 baht to US$1.

Throughout the country, money can be changed at banks, in larger hotels and currency exchange offices. By far the best rate is offered by bank counters in major tourist centres. They are usually open till late in the evening and sometimes at weekends. You will get better rates for travellers' cheques than cash. All major credit cards are widely accepted in Bangkok and main tourist centres. If used for shopping purposes, expect a surcharge of between 3 and 5 percent at some outlets. The Thai Farmers Bank, which has a wide network of branches, accepts up to five Eurocheques per month.

Tipping

Most up-market restaurants add a service charge to the bill, but in ordinary restaurants, tip the waiter at least 10 percent if you feel that you've been accorded good service.

Time

Thailand is seven hours ahead of Greenwich Mean Time,

but in Summer Time there is only a six-hour difference from the UK.

Electricity
Electricity is rated at 220 volts. In the simpler hotels, the sockets are often the flat American type.

Opening times
Banks: Monday to Friday, 8.30am–3.30pm.
Bureaux de change in the tourist centres: daily until at least 10pm.
Shops: there are no strict opening times, but many shops open from 8am–9pm. Department stores and shopping centres usually open at 10am.
Offices and government buildings: Monday to Friday, 8.30am–noon and 1–4.30pm. Arrangements to cover the lunch break vary.

Public holidays
Thai public holidays are as follows: 1 January (New Year), 6 April (Chakri Day), 13–15 April (Songkran, the Thai New Year Festival), 1 May (Labour Day), 5 May (Coronation Day), 12 August (Queen's Birthday), 23 October (Chulalongkorn Day), 5 December (King's Birthday) and 10 December (Constitution Day). Many shops may also close on Buddhist festivals *(see page 68)*.

Postal services
Most post offices are open from Monday to Friday, 8.30am–4.30pm and Saturday, 9am–noon. The General Post Office (GPO) in Charoen Krung Road and the post office in the departure hall at the international airport stay open for longer (Monday to Friday, 8am–8pm, Saturday and Sunday until 1pm).

It is possible to phone abroad or send faxes (ask for a special form) from most post offices. A packing service ensures all purchases are well packaged before being sent home. Air-mail postcards and letters for Europe take between four and 10 days. A courier service (EMS) is available for abroad and within Thailand.

Calling long-distance

Telephone, fax and cybercafés
A variety of private and public pay and phone card services make it easy to call locally and overseas – if the equipment is not out of order. Local calls from public phones cost 1 baht per three-minute unit. Overseas calls and faxes in hotels or business centres are generally expensive, but international calls by phone card are cheaper. Access AT&T at 001-999-11-111, Sprint: 001-999-13-877.

Cybercafes – in Ploenchit, Siam Square and Silom, for example – offer a popular means of staying in touch.

NB Internet, one of many in Khaosan Road (tel: 02-282 5619) does digital snapshots to 'post' as well as offering food and screen-quality videos for travellers in transit.

Newspapers

The *Bangkok Post* and *The Nation* are good English-language newspapers. For background information on political events in southeast Asia, consult either *Far Eastern Economic Review*, *Asia Week*, *Newsweek* or *Time*. Most hotels keep a supply of tourist magazines in their lounges.

Radio and TV

As well as the Thai radio and TV stations, there are a number of English-language cable channels, such as CNN and the BBC for news, entertainment from Hong Kong with Star Plus, Indian-style music on V and also a sports channel.

Photography

Thais love group photos in front of famous buildings and most people are happy to be photographed by foreigners. There are exceptions, however, and this should be remembered. Members of the royal family and the Emerald Buddha in the Wat Phra Kaeo must never be photographed. Visitors to other temples should also pay due respect.

What to wear

As the temperature in Bangkok rarely falls below 20°C (68°F) at night, light clothing, preferably cotton, is best. Until recently, restaurants, buses and hotels set their air-conditioning to a lower level, but now a jacket is rarely required. However, summer clothing should not be too casual or loose.

The Thais dress smartly

Thais judge strangers by their outward appearance and so set great store by smart dress. The upper arms should be covered and locals never wear shorts or swimming costumes away from the swimming pools or go-go bars. Visitors who arrive at the Royal Palace with shorts, sleeveless shirts or open-toe shoes will only be allowed in if they borrow some respectable clothing from the guards. All hotels provide a prompt laundry service with charges in direct proportion to the room price.

Etiquette

The traditional hospitality of the Thai people makes it easy for foreigners to make contact with them. Tourists usually receive a generous welcome and are treated with extreme courtesy. They are forgiven for inadvertently offending against Thai customs if they try to behave decently.

The presence of Western-style bars and restaurants does not alter the fact that visitors are in a Buddhist country with an ancient culture. Loud, arrogant behaviour injures the pride of the tradition-conscious Thais. Even if no-one remarks on it, tourists can be certain that they lose the approval of their hosts by disrespectful behaviour. Thais are patient and will probably smile even if they are not happy about things.

The royal family are considered to be above criticism. Any objects or pictures that represent the king are given an exalted position. The same applies to Buddha figures which stand as symbols for the people's faith.

Shows of affection in public are only permitted between men and men and between women and women. Among adults, the head, the most sacred part of the body, should not be touched. Similarly, never stretch out the foot, the lowest part of the body, towards another and certainly not towards a Buddha statue in a temple. It is also regarded as impolite to look down on someone else. When passing someone who is seated, always lower the head as a symbolic gesture.

Another problem for foreigners is the correct use of *wei*, the Thai greeting. This is not a handshake, but a prayer-like, palms-together gesture, and the height of the hands is determined by the status of the person being greeted. A slight nod of the head, not a handshake, is usually regarded as an acceptable greeting for Westerners to use.

Health precautions

Make sure that inoculations against polio and tetanus are carried out well before the departure date. The stress arising from the climatic changes, the time difference and strange food can induce some physical symptoms, so it is well worth taking it easy on the first day.

Thai food is usually prepared in hygienic conditions and is rarely responsible for stomach upsets, but it is wise to avoid street food, unpeeled fruit and vegetables and tap water if you are prone to upsets. Ice cubes can be a source of infection, as they are often made from impure water. Always drink plenty of liquid.

Malaria and other tropical diseases do not occur in Bangkok itself, but when travelling in the Kanchanaburi region and to Ko Samet take special precautions against mosquitoes (particularly at dusk), sleep under a mosquito net or in an air-conditioned room. Anyone intending to stay for longer periods should consider some sort of anti-malarial medication. For up-to-date information contact a hospital for tropical diseases in your country. If malaria is suspected, seek help in Bangkok from the Hospital for Tropical Diseases, Mahi-dol University, on Raj Withee Road, tel: (02) 246 12 72.

The monarchy is exalted: statue of Rama III

ONLY POLITE VISITORS ARE WELCOME

Tattoo shop

Chemists are well stocked

As a large number of prostitutes in Bangkok are HIV positive, there is a serious risk of contracting Aids. Many men clearly ignore this advice. Hepatitis B is not only passed on by sexual contact, but also by a tattooist's dirty needles, acupuncture treatment and injections. If an injection is required for a particular treatment, insist on a disposable needle. To counter the less dangerous hepatitis A virus, which can be passed on through food, a new, safer injection is now available.

Rabies is widespread in Thailand, so leave stray dogs and cats well alone. Seek medical assistance if bitten or scratched.

Medical treatment

The capital of Thailand has a large network of hospitals and private clinics, where many of the doctors speak English or were trained, at least in part, in Europe or the USA. Whereas treatment in a state-run hospital is free apart from a small admission charge, any services provided in the private clinics must be paid for in full. However, medical fees are much lower than in Europe. Prescribed medicines are dispensed directly by the clinics. Chemists stock most Western drugs, such as antibiotics, but they may well be sold under a different name, so anyone likely to need a particular medication is advised to keep a copy of the leaflet with details of the drug. As some of the medications in circulation are counterfeit, it is wise to bring a good supply of any prescribed medicine. It is recommended that travellers arrange a comprehensive overseas travel sickness insurance, including home transport if necessary.

Emergencies

Police, tel: 191
Fire brigade, tel: 199
Ambulance, tel: 281 15 44
Ambulance for accidents, tel: 252 2171-5
Tourist Service Centre, tel: 1155 (24-hour police emergency and tourist information service)
Suicide crisis intervention, tel: 662 09 79.

Shopping alert

Bangkok is well-known not just for the sale of pirated brand names, but also for fake antiques. Since 1989, trading in antiques in Thailand has been banned. Any such items may only be exported with the permission of the Fine Arts Department (tel: 02-221 7811).

The Weekend Market is notorious for its trade in rare species, outlawed by the CITES agreement. Any product made from a threatened species, such as crocodile leather bags, turtle-shell spectacles or ivory carvings comes within this law. Customs officers at home will prosecute.

Crime

The tourist police in Bangkok spend most of their time dealing with deception and theft. Crimes of violence are very rare. Valuables are best deposited in hotel or room safes. If the safe at the hotel reception does not have individual compartments, only leave travellers' cheques if the cheque numbers are recorded and kept separately. Credit cards should not be left either. The greatest risk of theft occurs on the busy urban buses, among the crowds at the markets and in night-clubs.

Victims of crime should always inform the police as soon as possible. Insurance companies will only pay compensation for stolen personal belongings if the theft is registered with the police and an official document issued. If a passport is stolen, a photocopy showing the entry visa stamp is very helpful to embassy staff as proof of identity. Stolen travellers' cheques will be replaced as long as proof of purchase and cheque numbers can be produced.

When it comes to buying drugs, foreigners are particularly vulnerable as often the sellers are police informers. Never agree to carry a parcel home for a passing acquaintance.

Police emergencies involving foreign visitors should be reported by calling 1155. The Tourism Authority of Thailand will relay your call to the English-speaking Tourist Police in Ratdamnoen Nok Road (near the Ratdamnoen Boxing Stadium). Well-trained and helpful staff will help you with the emergency.

Diplomatic representation

United Kingdom: 1031 N Wireless Road, Bangkok, tel: (02) 253 0191.
United States of America (consular offices): 95 Wireless Road, Bangkok, tel: (02) 205 4000.

There to assist

Accommodation

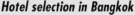

When choosing a hotel, consider the location. Few holidaymakers will wish to spend large amounts of time stuck in traffic jams. The hotels around Sukhumvit Road and Silom Road are ideal for those wishing to see the shops, eat well and join in the nightlife. Those more interested in Bangkok's cultural side do not have to stay in a hotel in the old town, although this part of the city certainly has its charm. Residents at the hotels near the river have easy access – via the express boats – to the city's cultural centre and Chinatown.

The choice of accommodation ranges from partitioned dormitories costing just a few pounds per night to luxurious suites in international-class hotels, where nothing is spared but the prices can be astronomical. Usually, the city has plenty of beds available and shortages occur only at Christmas and around the Chinese New Year. Out of season, even good quality hotels offer price reductions, especially if reservations are made through travel agents in Bangkok. Guests should, however, be aware that the dearer hotels add 10 percent for service and 7 percent for VAT. Staff also expect a tip in proportion to the room price.

To dial Bangkok from abroad, the prefix is 66 2, within Thailand 02.

92

The Shangri-La

The following hotel suggestions are listed according to three categories: $$$ = expensive; $$ = moderate; $ = inexpensive.

Hotel selection in Bangkok

$$$**Oriental**, 48 Oriental Avenue, tel: (02) 236 0400, fax: (02) 236 1937. Classic Bangkok hotel with its own river landing. $$$**The Peninsula**, 333 Charoen Nakorn Road, tel: (02) 861 1111, fax: (02) 861 1112. New riverside elegance. $$$**JW Marriott**, 4 Sukhum-vit Soi 2, tel: (02) 656 7700, fax: (02) 656 7711. $$$**Shangri-La**, 89 Soi Wat Suanplu, tel: (02) 236 7777, fax: (02) 236 8579. Modern hotel with a marvellous view of the river from its lobby and all of its 800 rooms. Own landing stage. $$$**Royal Orchid Sheraton**, 2 Captain Bush Lane, Si Phaya Road, tel: (02) 234 5599, fax: (02) 236 8320. A luxury hotel by the Si Phaya Pier with a large terrace, two swimming pools and an adjoining shopping centre. $$$**The Dusit Thani**, 946 Rama IV Road, tel: (02) 238 4790, fax: (02) 238 4797. Unalloyed luxury at the end of Silom Road, opposite Lumpini Park. Those who wish to keep fit can take part in the early morning sports programme. $$$**Grand Hyatt Erawan**, 494 Ratdamri Road, tel: (02) 254 1234, fax: (02) 253 5856. Impressive new building, situated at the central junction of the shopping centre. The Erawan Shrine

is the hotel's spirit house. **$$$Royal Princess**, 269 Lan Luang Road, tel: (02) 281 3088, fax: (02) 280 1314. This, the only luxury hotel in the old centre, is set back from the road between two-storey residential and business premises. Good restaurant. **$$$The Beaufort Sukothai**, 13/3 Sathorn Tai Road, tel: (02) 287 0222, fax: (02) 287 4980. Thai tradition but in an up-to-date style. A successful amalgamation of silk and granite. Something for the aesthete.

$$Ambassador, 171 Sukhumvit Road, tel: (02) 254 04 44, fax: (02) 253 41 23. In the Sukhumvit Road hotel area. Over 1,000 comfortable rooms in various categories. Several popular restaurants. **$$Asia Hotel**, Phaya Thai Road, tel: (02) 215 0808, fax: (02) 215 4360. Popular hotel with tour group. Rooftop swimming pool. Under German management. **$$The Park**, 6 Sukhumvit Road, Soi 7, tel: (02) 255 4300, fax: (02) 255 4309. Quiet hotel in a central location. **$$Swissotel**, 3 Convent Road, tel: (02) 233 5345, fax: (02) 236 9425. Convenient business location. Nice swimming pool. **$$Tower Inn**, 533 Silom Road, tel: (02) 237 8300, fax: (02) 237 8286. Fantastic view from the roof garden. **$$Rembrandt Hotel**, Sukhumvit Road, Soi 18, tel: (02) 261 7100, fax: (02) 261 7017. Excellent value and a good position for shopping and nightlife. Swimming pool and restaurants; its Indian restaurant currently ranks as the best in the city. **$$Quality Hotel Pinnacle**, 17 Soi Ngam Duphli, tel: (02) 287 0111, fax: (02) 287 3420. Modern business hotel belonging to an international chain, near Lumpini Park. **$$Viengtai**, 42 Tani Road, tel: (02) 280 5434, fax: (02) 281 8153. A medium category hotel in the heart of the bustling Banglampoo quarter. **$$YMCA Collins**, 27 Sathorn Tai Road, tel: (02) 287 1900, fax: (02) 287 1996. Modern hotel popular with long-stay tourists. **$$Manohra**, 412 Suriwong Road, tel: (02) 234 5070, fax: (02) 237 7662. Older hotel in the jewellers' district. **$$Royal**, 2 Ratdamnoen Klang Road, tel: (02) 222 9111, fax: (02) 224 2083. A very popular hotel thanks to its central location by the Sanam Luang. Well-furnished rooms, swimming pool. **$$YWCA**, 13 Sathorn Tai Road, tel: (02) 286 1936, fax: (02) 287 3016. Simple and cheaper than the YMCA.

$City Lodge, Sukhumvit Road, Soi 9, tel: (02) 253 7705, fax: (02) 255 4667. Also Sukhumvit Road, Soi 19, tel: 254 4783, fax: (02) 255 7340. Ideal for those who prefer a smaller hotel.

Economical alternatives

Guesthouses can be found everywhere in the city, but they are chiefly concentrated in Khaosan Road and its side

Khaosan Road guesthouse

streets in the centre of the old town. Anyone unhappy with the hustle and bustle will find alternatives further west between the Wat Chai Chana Songkhram and the Phra Athit pier, and further north in Thewet. There are plenty more guesthouses in Soi Ngam Duphli near Lumpini Park.

Hotel selection outside Bangkok

Ayutthaya
$$Krung Si River, 27/2 Moo 11 Rojana Road, tel: (035) 42996. This new, comfortable hotel lies to the south of the station next to the road bridge over the Menam Pasak. **$$Ayutthaya Grand**, 55/5 Rojana Road, tel: (035) 335483, fax: (035) 335492. Swimming pool. 4km (2.5 miles) outside the town, by the bus station. **$$U Thong Inn**, 210 Rojana Road, tel: (035) 242236, fax: (035) 24 22 35. Simple tourist hotel, in a rather remote spot.

Kanchanaburi
$$$Felix River Kwai Resort, 9/1 Moo 3, Tha Makham, tel: (034) 515061, fax: (034) 515095. Luxurious resort hotel situated in spacious grounds by the river, north of the bridge. **$$River Kwai Hotel**, 284/4–6 Saengchuto Road, tel: (034) 511184, fax: (035) 511269. Large business hotel in the town centre. **$$River Kwai Village Hotel**, Ban Phu Ta Kien by the Kwae Noi, tel: (034) 591055. Comfortable resort hotel in attractive countryside, by the river. **$$River Kwai Cabin**, beneath the Wang Po viaduct, tel: (02) 412 4509. Simple accommodation on the river. **$Rick's Lodge**, 45/3 Ban Nove, tel: (034) 514831. Small guesthouse. Simple rooms with shower and WC.

Sofitel Central

Hua Hin
$$$Sofitel Central, 1 Damnoen Kasem Road, tel: (032) 512021-38, fax: (032) 511014. Traditional hotel with restored, colonial-style bungalows and rooms. **$$$Melia**, Naresdamri Road, tel: (032) 511612-4, fax: (032) 511135. Modern premises by the beach. **$$Royal Garden Village**, 43/1 Petchkasem Road, tel: (032) 520250-6, fax: (032) 476 1120. Luxurious, Thai-style bungalows in attractive grounds. By the sea, 5km (3 miles) north of the town.

Dusit Resort

Pattaya
$$$Royal Cliff Beach Resort, 353 Moo 12, Cliff Road, tel: (038) 421421-30, fax: (038) 428511. 900 rooms by a private bay with sandy beach, four swimming pools and every luxury. **$$$Dusit Resort**, 240 Pattaya Beach Road, tel: (038) 429901-33, fax: (038) 428239. Stylish, luxury resort hotel on the northern shore. Large, spacious rooms. **$$Thai Garden Resort**, 179/168 Moo 5, North Pattaya Road, tel: (038) 426009, fax: (038) 426198. Family-orientated complex away from the town centre.

Index